# Unconventional Survival: Bag Essentials

A Survivalist's Guide for Creatively Repurposing Everyday Items Found in a Bag

By: Galilani Ahawi

The material and information contained in this book is for general information purposes only. You should not solely rely upon the material or information in the book as a basis for making any decisions. This book makes no representations or warranties of any kind, express or implied, about the completeness, accuracy, reliability, suitability or availability with respect to the information, products, services or related graphics contained in the book for any purpose. Any reliance you place on such material is therefore strictly at your own risk.



Printed in the United States of America

First Paperback Edition: March 2024

ISBN: 979-8-9903042-0-8


Self-Published
https://poplme.co/archeryempress/share

# ABOUT YOUR SURVIVAL INSTRUCTOR

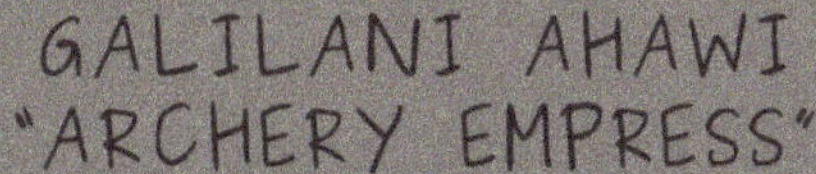

As a lover of nature and outdoor recreation, I teach women the art of rustic & urban survival through one-on-one classes, exclusive events, and short, informative videos. With the idea of holistic totality in mind, I leverage my Bachelor of Science degree in Dietetics to emphasize the significance of natural living and understanding nutrition, health, and alternative healing from a survivalist's perspective. My mission is to awaken warrior goddesses and introduce them to a world of survival, self-reliance, and preparedness.

## NOTE TO READER

This book is filled with unconventional applications for everyday items. The examples presented here are merely a starting point to inspire your own creativity. Don't hesitate to explore new ways to use these items in ways that may not have been mentioned in this book. The possibilities are endless!

SCAN FOR MORE INFO

# Disclaimer

The publisher and author offer this book and its contents on an "as is" basis, without making any representations or warranties regarding the book or its contents. They disclaim all such representations and warranties, including but not limited to warranties of healthcare, skill, personal safety, and Survivability. Furthermore, they take no responsibility for any errors, inaccuracies, omissions, or inconsistencies found within. The author and publisher do not guarantee the accuracy, completeness, or timeliness of the information provided in this book.

The publisher and the author make no guarantees concerning the level of success you may experience by following the advice and strategies contained in this book, and you accept the risk that results will differ for each individual. The testimonials and examples provided in this book show exceptional results, which may not apply to the average reader, and are not intended to represent or guarantee that you will achieve the same or similar results. It is recommended to seek advice from a legal or qualified professional regarding the suggestions and recommendations in this book. Except where explicitly stated, neither the author nor the publisher, nor any contributors or representatives mentioned in the book, will be held liable for any damages resulting from the use of this book. This limitation of liability covers all types of damages, including compensatory, direct, indirect, consequential damages, loss of life, property damage, or claims from third parties.

The supplements, nutraceuticals, amino acids, essential oils, fatty acids, probiotics, and other items listed in this work are examples of functional foods and how they can be used to help, support, promote, and maintain different ailments and the symptoms associated with said ailments. The information, including but not limited to, text, graphics, images, and other material contained in this book are for informational purposes only and is not intended to diagnose, treat, cure, or prevent any condition or disease. It is important to note that this book is not a substitute for professional advice from a licensed legal, healthcare, or other professional. Always consult with a licensed professional to ensure you are making the best decisions for your specific situation. By using this book, you acknowledge and accept this disclaimer.

# Preface

Greetings intrepid reader,

Within the pages of this guidebook lies a treasury of knowledge that transcends the ordinary and equips you with the extraordinary. As we navigate the unpredictable tapestry of life, there comes a moment when ingenuity becomes the key to survival. This book is your passport to a world where everyday items transform into instruments of resilience and resourcefulness.

In your hands now is a compendium of unconventional survival skills, a guide that unveils the hidden potential in the commonplace. From the mundane to the extraordinary, this collection will empower you to repurpose the tools of your daily existence in ways you never imagined.

Whether you find yourself lost in the wilderness, facing the unexpected challenges of urban living, or simply desiring a touch of resourcefulness in your everyday routine, this guide is your steadfast companion. It unfolds a tapestry of techniques that go beyond the conventional, offering you insights into harnessing the power of common objects for your survival and well-being.

As you embark on this journey through the art of unconventional resourcefulness, remember that knowledge is the ultimate tool in your arsenal. This guide is designed to be your beacon, illuminating the path toward self-reliance and inventive problem-solving.

May the wisdom contained within these pages serve as a guide, inspiring you to view the world through a lens of possibility. Embrace the unexpected, discover the extraordinary in the ordinary, and let this guide be your compass in navigating the uncharted territories of unconventional survival.

Safe travels and resourceful adventures!

Sincerely, GA

"You have everything that you need to survive within you; just be creative and kick life's ass in your own way."

—Galilani Ahawi

Scan the QR Code to access how-to videos demonstrating the unconventional uses of these items across various social media platforms.

# Table of Contents

## 1 FOOD



## 5 BEVERAGES

# Table of Contents

# Table of Contents

## 18 BEAUTY



## 23 MEDICAL SUPPLIES

# Table of Contents

## 27 OFFICE SUPPLIES



## 31 BABY

# Table of Contents

## 34 TOOLS



## 37 CLOTHING

# Table of Contents

## 40 OTHER ITEMS

## 41 OTHER ITEMS

# Table of Contents

## 42 OTHER ITEMS

## 43 OTHER ITEMS

# Table of Contents

## 44 HELPFUL TIPS



## 47 FOR YOUR INFORMATION



## 49 MORSE CODE



## 51 NOTES

# Food

## Gum

Stress Reliever

Chewing gum helps improve stress and negative mood by reducing cortisol.

Target Practice

Chewing gum helps keep nerves calm and focused when aiming at targets by improving concentration.

Fishing Aid

Gum with added sugar and coloring attracts certain types of fish, including small fish like minnows, commonly used to catch larger fish.

Aids Digestion

Chewing gum increases saliva production, which can stimulate intestinal activity and ease upset stomach, nausea, and vomiting.

Oral Health

Gum increases saliva production, which can reduce plaque and tooth decay.

Appetite & Thirst Suppressant

Menthol from mint flavoring influences thirst, and chewing helps short-term appetite regulation.

Emergency Sealant

Temporarily fix holes, tears, or breaks in glass, plastic, or fabric.

Start a Fire

To ignite a fire, cut a gum wrapper with a thinner middle section. Hold the aluminum wrapper on each side of a charged battery's terminals. Then, touch the tinder to the center of the foil wrapper to ignite.

## Other Uses

_______________________________

_______________________________

_______________________________

_______________________________

## Chocolate

Topical Uses

Cocoa helps protect against harmful UV damage, provides hydration, helps treat skin diseases, and improves blood circulation.

Mosquito Repellant

It is believed that the aroma of caramelized chocolate helps to hinder mosquitoes from detecting carbon dioxide on your breath.

Nutritional & Medicinal Benefits

Chocolate helps reduce menstrual symptoms, improves stress and anxiety, boosts energy, improves blood flow, and benefits the heart, brain, and immune system.

## Other Uses

_______________________________

_______________________________

_______________________________

_______________________________

# Food



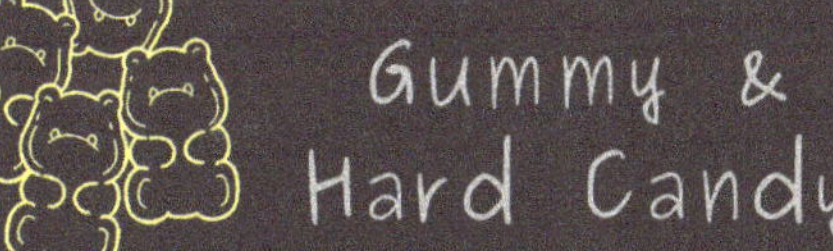

## Gummy & Hard Candy

Emergency Sealant

Melt candy and use the sticky substance to temporarily fix holes, tears, or breaks in glass, plastic, and fabric.

Lure Your Next Meal

Use candy as a lure to trap animals or insects looking to satisfy their sweet tooth.

Energy

Certain candies provide a quick burst of energy that lasts for a few minutes.

Mood Booster

Candy helps boost morale in stressful situations.

Distraction from Hunger & Thirst

Mastication and salivation can reduce appetite, cravings, and thirst.

Weapon (Hard Candy)*

Candy can be used in three ways: broken into tiny shards, sharpened to a point for a spear or arrowhead, or used as a projectile for a slingshot.

## Mint Candy

Health Benefits

Peppermint may help reduce nausea and abdominal pain from GI tract issues.

## Hot Sauce

Antimicrobial

Spices such as cumin can provide antimicrobial benefits.

Animal & Insect Repellent

Many animals hate the heat from capsaicin. Use hot sauce as a way to keep pests away.

Self-Defense*

Use hot sauce as an alternative to pepper spray for self-protection.

Topical Pain Reliever

Capsaicin, when applied topically, can be used to help relieve neuropathic pain.

Nutritional & Medicinal Benefits

Capsaicin aids in weight loss, decreases inflammation, and can slow the growth of cancer cells.

## Tamarind Candy

Nutritional & Medicinal Benefits

Tamarind has anticancer, antioxidant, and anti-inflammatory properties. It helps boost the immune system, lowers blood glucose levels, and benefits the heart, liver, bowel, joints, and brain.

Topical Uses

Tamarind seed extract contains potential antiaging effects.

Gelling Agent & Stabilizer

Decorticated tamarind seed kernels are used to make pectin. Pectin thickens and stabilizes food, enabling the mixture of oil and water.

# Food

## Other Uses

______________________

______________________

______________________

______________________

## Meat Snacks

Emergency Straw

Hollow out a meat stick and use it as a makeshift straw.

Lure Your Next Meal

Use meat snacks as a lure to hunt, fish, and trap animals or insects.

## Baby Formula

Emergency Nutrition Source

During emergency situations, it's worth remembering that baby formula can be used as an alternative source of nutrition for adults.

## Sour Candy

Nutritional & Medicinal Benefits

Citric Acid helps protect against kidney stones, increases nutrient absorption, and helps metabolize energy.

Other Uses for Citric Acid

The sour powder from certain sour candies can be used to preserve food and remove stains.

## Baked/Fried Snacks

Trail Marker

Use snacks as temporary trail markers in the event that you get lost.

Water Collection

Use the packaging to collect water.

Storage

Use the packaging to store items.

Dishware

Use the packaging as dishware to hold food or beverages.

Lure Your Next Meal

Use snacks as a lure to hunt, fish, and trap animals or insects.

Candle

Ignite greasy snacks on fire and use them as a temporary light source.

Faucet

Poke holes in the snack packaging and add water to create a steady stream of H2O.

Water Filter

Make a water filter by using snack packaging as the base. Layer cotton or fabric, sand, charcoal, and rocks of different sizes (small to large) in that sequence for the internal setup.

## Other Uses

______________________

______________________

______________________

______________________

# Food

## Salt (Sodium Chloride)

Nutritional & Medicinal Benefits

Salt is an electrolyte that carries nutrients into cells, maintains fluid balance, supports muscle movement, regulates blood pressure, and supports brain and gastric performance.

Exfoliant

Add salt to soap and use the mixture to scrub away dead skin.

Ant Repellant

Place a line of salt where you don't want ants to cross to help keep them away.

Kills Poison Ivy

Add salt to soapy water and spray the mixture to help kill poison ivy.

Saline Solution

Mix 8 tsp salt and 1 gallon distilled water to make saline. It is used to hydrate mucous membranes, clean wounds, and treat dehydration.

Respiratory Aid

Gargling with salt water can help reduce upper respiratory infections.

Preserve Food

Use salt to extend the life of food for prolonged periods.

Rust Cleaner

Make a paste from salt and water and use it to scrub the rust off of surfaces.

Treat Sore Throat

Gargle with salt water to help ease a sore throat.

Treat Minor Cuts & Insect Bites

A topical application of salt can increase the effectiveness of wound healing from bites and minor cuts.

Clean Your Mouth

Gargling with salt water can help maintain oral health.

## Black Licorice Candy Sticks

Emergency Straw

Bite the ends off of a hollow piece of licorice and use it as an emergency straw.

Curb Sugar Cravings

Licorice root is naturally sweet-tasting. Use it as a sugar alternative.

Livestock Health Benefits

Licorice root offers health benefits for livestock, and by extension, for you as well.

Nutritional & Medicinal Benefits

Licorice has antioxidant, anti-inflammatory, anticarcinogenic, antiviral, and antiulcer effects. It improves digestion, reduces inflammation, treats upper respiratory problems, and benefits skin and oral health.

## Ginger Candy

Nutritional & Medicinal Benefits

Ginger is an antiemetic, anti-inflammatory, and anticancer agent. It also reduces cholesterol and promotes healthy skin and teeth.

Pest Repellant

Ginger extract is an effective insecticide against ants, flies, roaches, and mosquitoes.

## Pepper

Nutritional & Medicinal Benefits

Pepper is an antioxidant, antimicrobial, and anti-inflammatory. It is also gastro & neuroprotective and has antidepressant effects.

Temporarily Stop Minor Radiator Leaks

When you have identified a leak, pour pepper into the radiator of a cooled engine to stop further leaking. (Caution: may damage your cooling system.)

# Beverages

## Soda

### Cola Uses:

- Removes grease and blood stains from fabric and other surfaces
- Removes rust and burnt-on mess
- Prevents tarnishing
- Helps strip paint off metal (takes a few days)
- Repels, traps, and kills bugs such as aphids, arthropods, & gastropods
- Gardening aid
  - Can be used as a fertilizer (1 part cola, 3 parts water)
  - Composting booster
- Gets Rid of limescale
- May help soothe asthma attacks (caffeine)
- Defrosts glass
- Cleans car battery terminals and headlights
- Surface cleaner (non-disinfectant)
- Helps remove gum from hair
- Caffeine at low doses can help your memory, brain, and cognitive function
- Helps to boost energy levels
- Sugar alternative for cooking
- Helps get rid of skunk odor
- Mentos & cola explosion (distraction)
- Mix milk & soda to curdle milk

### Soda Water Uses:

- Cleans fabrics and surfaces
- Helps nourish plants
- Carbonation helps to improve your swallowing ability, increase satiety, and relieve constipation
- Add to recipes to enhance delicacy

### Uses for Other Types of Soda:

- Flavors food
- Dyes white fabrics

## Juice

### Citrus Uses:

- Fights Odors
- Helps repel mosquitoes
- Cleans
  - Helps remove limescale, rust, soap residues, and hard water stains

### 100% Juice

The pulp from 100% juice can be used for organic composting.

### Other Juice Uses:

- Dye fabrics using juice that contains bold natural coloring or added food coloring
- Lure bugs and small animals

## Water

### Start a Fire

Use a filled water bottle to focus the sun's rays and start a fire on tinder.

### Coolant

Water can be used as a substitute coolant in air conditioning systems.

### Respiratory Aid

Boil water and inhale the steam to help relieve respiratory distress.

## Side Note:

### Drinks Full of Sugar

Boil sugary drinks until the liquid has reduced to a thick syrup, soft candy, or hard candy. Results may vary depending on cook time. Helpful tip: molten candy can be used as an emergency sealant or glue.

# Beverages



## Tea

Herbal Tea Health Benefits:

- Contains polyphenol antioxidants
- May reduce the risk of developing chronic diseases such as cancer, cardiovascular diseases, arthritis, and diabetes (Khan N, Tea and Health: Studies in Humans, 2013).
- May help with weight loss
- Helps to boost your energy

## Alcohol

Red Wine Vinegar

Make RWV with 1 part raw apple cider vinegar and 2 parts red wine. Cover with a cloth. Ferment the mixture at room temperature for approx. 2–6 weeks. Check regularly for a translucent, gelatinous disk (vinegar mother) and no mold formation. Strain. Store in an airtight container. Note: ACV is made when approx. 4 cut apples, 2 cups warm water, and 2 tbsp sugar sit for approx. 2 weeks in a cheesecloth-covered sterilized jar.

Compost

Due to its sugar content, you can use wine to activate compost.

Makeshift Dye

Dye fabrics with red wine.

Repel/Trap Bugs & Soothe Bites

Liquor can repel bugs and soothe bites. Wine can lure bugs into a trap.

Medicine

Use hard liquor as a base to make medicine such as tinctures.

Start a Fire

Easily start a fire using alcohol.

Disinfectant

Disinfect your skin, items, and surfaces with hard liquor.

First Aid

Use hard liquor to sterilize a wound and ease pain.

## Aloe Drinks

Topical Benefits

Crush the aloe pieces into a gel and use it topically for:

- Sunburn or other burns
- Protecting and moisturizing skin and hair
- Improving wound healing

Nutritional & Medicinal Benefits:

- Natural Laxative
- May improve oral health by helping to reduce plaque
- Antioxidant rich

## Coffee

Neutralize Odors

Coffee can help mask the smell of bad odors.

Pest Repellant

Use coffee and coffee grounds to help repel pests such as mosquitoes, flies, fleas, slugs, snails, and beetles.

Garden Aid

Coffee can be used as fertilizer and compost to promote plant growth.

Hair, Skin, & Nails

When applied topically, coffee can nourish and exfoliate skin as well as promote hair growth.

Natural Dye

Use coffee as a natural dye for fabrics.

Promote Mushroom Growth

Use coffee grounds as a medium to grow mushrooms.

Tenderize Meat

Use coffee grounds to tenderize meat.

Nutritional & Medicinal Benefits:

- Helps to boost energy levels
- May support brain & heart health
- May lower the risk of depression

# Beverages

## Dairy Products

### How to Make Yogurt

Ingredients: 1 quart milk and 1/4 cup premade yogurt (Scale up or down if needed)

Directions: Heat the milk to 180–210 degrees Fahrenheit. Cool the milk to 110–115 degrees Fahrenheit. Stir in the pre-made yogurt to add bacteria. Incubate in a lukewarm area for 4–9 hours. Refrigerate.

### How to Make Cheese

Ingredients: 4 cups milk, 2.5 tbsp lemon juice, and salt to taste

Directions: Heat milk on medium heat. Stir to avoid scorching. Add lemon juice when milk comes to a boil. Let it separate. Strain to separate solids from liquid. Whip solids until creamy.

### How to Make Heavy Whipping Cream

Ingredients: Milk and butter

Directions: Blend together 2/3 cup milk and 1/3 cup of melted butter.

### How to Make Butter & Buttermilk

Ingredients: Heavy whipping cream

Directions: Blend heavy whipping cream until fat separates from liquid. The solid is butter; the liquid is buttermilk.

### How to Make Milk Powder

Ingredients: Milk and lemon juice

Directions: Mix lemon juice with milk to separate solids from liquid. Dehydrate the curds to form the powder.

### Topical Uses:

- Helps relieve sunburn
- Helps relieve bug bites
- Softens skin

### Neutralize Spicy Food

Casein protein in milk breaks down the fatty acid bonds in capsaicin.

### Cleaning Uses:

- Removes ink stains from fabric
- Polishes silverware
- Cleans leather

## Coconut

### IV Fluid

Sterile coconut water from a healthy, unopened coconut can be used intravenously as a short-term IV fluid.

### Replenish Electrolytes

Coconut water is full of electrolytes that can help with muscle cramps, regulating blood pressure, supporting the nervous system, and keeping you hydrated.

### Fire Fuel

Blend freshly cut coconut flesh with water, let it sit for a few hours to separate (cream will be on the top and water on the bottom), place it in a cool place to harden the cream, separate and cook the hardened cream on medium heat until the curds separate and are slightly brown. Strain the fluid (oil) and use it to fuel your fire.

### MCT Oil

Coconuts contain healthy fats known as medium-chain triglycerides that can help with losing weight, fighting yeast and bacterial growth, maintaining blood sugar, supporting metabolism, and is an immediate source of energy.

### Oral Care

Coconut can be used in many ways to promote a healthy mouth.

### Activated Charcoal

WARNING

FLAMMABLE

To make a weak variation of activated charcoal yourself, heat coconut shells in a lid-covered pot for 3–5 hours. Then, rinse the ashes, dry them for 24 hours, and crush them into a powder. Next, mix 1 cup of lemon juice with 8 oz of ashes, soak them for 24 hours, and dehydrate them on high heat for 3+ hours. Activated Charcoal can be used to help filter air and water, reduce gas and diarrhea, and aid in eliminating toxins from the body.

# Beverage Containers



## Tea Bags

Eliminate Odor

Use a tea bag to help neutralize odors.

Garden Aid

Use a tea bag as organic fertilizer to support plant and mushroom growth.

Makeshift Dye

By steeping tea bags in water, you can create a natural dye that ranges from a light tan to a dark brown, depending on the ratio of water to tea.

Hair, Skin, & Nails

The herbs in tea bags can be used topically to promote healthy hair, skin, and nails.

Clean Surfaces

The herbs in tea bags can be used to clean, degrease, and shine surfaces.

Relieve Swollen Gums

Bite down on a tea bag after a tooth extraction to help swollen gums.

Absorbent Sponge

Use a tea bag to absorb moisture.

First Aid

Use a tea bag to help soothe sunburn, poison ivy rash, and bug bites.

Start a Fire

Use a dry tea bag to help start a fire.

## Juice Box Carton

Planter

Use a juice carton as a way to plant starter seeds.

Dishware

Open a drink carton and use it as reusable dishware.

## Glass

Small Game Feeder

Fill a glass bottle with acorns, nuts, and seeds to lure and capture small animals.

Torch

Fill a glass bottle with fuel, such as oil or alcohol. Saturate a cloth wick with the combustible fuel. Add the wick to the bottle, ignite it, and use it as a light source.

Greenhouse for Plants

Use a glass bottle as a makeshift greenhouse to promote the growth of seeds and seedlings.

Distill Water

To purify contaminated or salt water, connect two bottles (one filled with water and the other empty) and boil the water over a fire. Once all the water evaporates from the first bottle, you can safely drink the condensed water vapor collected in the connected bottle.

Alarm

Use a glass bottle to alert you when individuals are in close proximity by listening for shattering glass.

Cook Food

Cook food or boil water in a glass bottle over a campfire.

## Paper Cup

Compost

Add a shredded paper cup to enhance your compost.

Start a Fire

Paper cups can be used to easily start a fire.

Transplant Ready Planter

To transplant a seedling, plant it directly into the ground while it remains in the cup.

Wind Guard

Use a paper cup as a wind guard to protect a candle from blowing out.

# Beverage Containers

## Aluminum Can

### EMF Blocking Cage

Use a soda can as a way to help block RFID signals and protect your electronic items and credit cards.

### Makeshift Stove & Cookware

Create a stove or cookware from an empty soda can by lighting flammable material inside the can. Utilize it as a source of light, for warmth, or to prepare meals.

### Makeshift Cutting Tools*

Cut a can into shards and use the sharp pieces as makeshift knives or arrowheads.

### Reflective Surface

To start fires or signal for help using sunlight, create a reflective surface by buffing, cleaning, and polishing a can until it shines.

### Concealed Storage

Store items in a can to provide a perfect hideaway for small items.

### Fishing Hook

Transform a can tab into a fishing hook by snipping, shaping, sharpening, and tying it onto a line to catch fish.

## Foam

### Makeshift AC

Add ice to a foam container and use a fan to blow the cool air coming from inside the container into the surrounding area.

### Fishing Bobber

Use foam as the floating bobber for a fishing line.

### Stuffing

Crush foam into small pieces and use it as stuffing in items such as pillows, seat cushions, or coats.

## Straw

### Medicine Dropper

Use a straw as a way to measure and dispense liquids in small, precise increments.

### Spoon

Use a straw as a way to scoop substances.

### Candle

Stuff an eco-friendly straw full of cotton and a fuel such as petroleum jelly, and light it to create a prolonged source of fire.

### Waterproof Storage

Use an eco-friendly straw as a way to waterproof and hold small items by filling it and melting the ends together to create an enclosed capsule.

### Snorkel

Use a straw as an emergency snorkel.

### Whistle

Flatten an unbent straw, then cut one end into a triangular point. Blow into the cut end.

## Foam

### Sound Amplifier

Use a foam cup to enhance the clarity of a faint sound.

### Insulation

Use a foam cup to help keep things warm or cool.

### Create "Glue"/Pseudo Plastic

You can create a makeshift adhesive or soft plastic-like material by dipping foam into 100% acetone. The ratio of acetone to foam will determine the final result.

acetone>foam= glue-like substance

acetone<foam= plastic-like material

# Beverage Containers



## Other Uses

______________________________

______________________________

______________________________

______________________________

## Plastic Bottle

Water Still

Add non-toxic vegetation to a bottle, then leave the bottle in the sun to allow it to "sweat". The condensed water vapor produced is safe to drink.

Makeshift Shoes

Flatten two water bottles and use them to make the soles of makeshift shoes.

Fish Catcher

Unscrew the bottle cap. Cut and detach the bottle 1/4th from the top. Place bait in the bigger bottom piece. Then, place the smaller piece, capside first, into the bigger piece and put it in the water to trap small fish.

Water Filter

Make a water filter by using a water bottle as the base. Layer cotton or fabric, sand, charcoal, and rocks of different sizes (small to large) in that sequence for the internal setup.

Flotation Aid

Use empty bottles to create a makeshift flotation device.

Eye Protection

Make emergency eye protection by cutting a bottle in half lengthwise and using it as a shield.

Makeshift Greenhouse

Use a water bottle as a greenhouse to grow seeds into seedlings.

Funnel

Remove the cap from a water bottle, then cut the bottle in half and detach it to create a funnel for liquids.

Cordage

To make cordage from a bottle, use a sharp knife to create a slit at one end of the bottle. Then, carefully glide the knife in a continuous spiral around the length of the bottle by spinning it until it reaches the other end.

Waterproof Storage Container

Store small items in a water bottle.

Dishware

Cut a bottle in half and use the severed halves as dishware to consume food.

Faucet

Poke holes in the bottom of a bottle. Then, add water to create a steady stream of H2O.

Lantern

Use a bottle as a wind protector for a candle/torch, or add water to a bottle to amplify the light from a smaller light source, such as a flashlight.

Makeshift Gas Mask

Use a liter or gallon bottle as a makeshift gas mask by cutting the bottle to fit around your face. Create an airtight seal around your face. Remove the cap. Squish cotton/fabric and charcoal in the narrow cap opening to help filter air.

# Toiletries

## Other Uses

______________________________

______________________________

______________________________

______________________________

______________________________

______________________________

## Lotion

Emergency Lubricant

Use lotion as a way to minimize friction and allow smooth movement.

## Tampon

Storage & Concealment

Use tampon packaging and applicators to store small objects.

Seed Starter

Germinate seeds by separating the cotton from a tampon, adding seeds, and watering the mixture.

Insulation

Use a tampon as a way to keep warm by unraveling the cotton and using it to insulate socks and gloves.

Emergency Cordage

A tampon string can be used as emergency cordage by unraveling it to expose the smaller strands. The strands can then be tied or braided together to create a long cord.

Tinder

The cotton material of a tampon can easily be ignited to start a fire.

Water Filter

Use a tampon to strain and dispense water from a makeshift water filter.

First Aid

A tampon can be used as a bandage, compress, or gauze.

Oral Care

Use a clean tampon as a way to clean and floss teeth.

Candle Wick

Use a tampon as an improvised wick for a candle or lantern.

Water Collection

Collect water by using a tampon to absorb and transfer it from one place to another.

Emergency Straw

A tampon applicator can be used as a straw to get water from hard-to-reach places.

Ear & Nose Plug

Use tampons as a plug to protect your nose and ears.

Bottle Cork

Use a tampon to cork a bottle.

Semi-Hard Plastic Uses

Repurpose the applicator by melting it, using eco-friendly methods, and molding it into useful items, or use the molten plastic as a makeshift glue.

Lure or Bait

Saturate a tampon in blood or food to lure animals into a trap.

# Toiletries



## Sanitary Napkin

Emergency Face Mask

Use a pad as a face mask to help filter harmful fumes or particles in the air.

Seed Starter

Use a sanitary napkin to germinate seeds by placing the seeds on the absorbent pad and adding water.

Water Filter

Materials such as cotton used to make sanitary napkins can help filter water from harmful debris.

First Aid

A sanitary napkin can be used as a bandage, compress, or gauze.

Oven Mitts

Sanitary napkins can act as oven mitts, allowing you to pick up hot items.

Emergency Footwear

Sanitary napkins can be used to make the soles of makeshift shoes.

Insulation

Insulate clothing, socks, and gloves with sanitary napkins to help keep you warm in emergencies.

Sponge

Utilize a sanitary napkin in various applications, including bathing, cleaning, or transferring fluids.

Lure or Bait

Saturate a pad in blood or food to lure animals into a trap.

Start a Fire

The cotton within a pad can easily be ignited with just a spark.

Emergency Tape or Patch

Use the sticky side of a pad to temporarily bond or join objects together.

## Tissue Paper

Mark Your Path

Use torn pieces of tissue to mark your path for an easy way to map out your location.

Emergency Measuring Device

Use tissues as a quick reference for length when measuring items.

Sponge

Utilize tissue in various applications, including bathing, cleaning, or transferring fluids.

Start a Fire

Use tissues to easily ignite a fire.

Garden Aid

Use damp tissue paper to sprout seeds or grow mushrooms.

## Perfume

Fire Fuel

Use this flammable liquid to start a fire.

Emergency Sanitizer

The alcohol content in perfume can be used as a weak emergency sanitizer.

Why Cleansing a Wound is Not Advised

While it may seem logical that the alcohol content in perfume could aid in disinfecting a wound, it is not recommended due to the presence of other ingredients.

## Other Uses

______________________________

______________________________

______________________________

______________________________

# Toiletries

## Other Uses

______________________________

______________________________

______________________________

______________________________

## Dental Floss

Emergency Sutures
Use unflavored dental floss and a sterile needle to stitch a wound.

Emergency Thread
Use dental floss as a way to stitch and repair items.

Fishing Line or Net
Floss can be used as a fishing line or knitted together to create a makeshift fishing net.

Rope/Cording
Dental floss can be used as a rope to complete tasks such as tying, fixing, hoisting, etc.

Shoestrings
Dental floss can be used as emergency shoestrings.

Improvised Cutting Tool
Dental floss can be used to cut through soft items such as bread.

Start a Fire
Woven dental floss made from cotton can be used to start a fire.

Pony Tail Holder
Keep your hair out of your face by using floss as a hair tie.

## Deodorant

Insect Control
Deodorant made with ingredients such as tea tree oil can act as a bug repellent or provide relief for insect bites. (Avoid broken skin.)

Survival Candle
Coconut and other natural oil-based deodorants can be transformed into impromptu candles by adding a wick and igniting a flame.

Prevent Blistering & Chafing
To prevent blisters from forming, you can use deodorant to reduce surface friction.

Get Rid of Moisture
Apply deodorant to areas of the body, such as your hands, feet, or underarms, to prevent moisture build-up.

Emergency Lubricant
Use deodorant as a way to minimize friction and allow smooth movement.

## Other Uses

______________________________

______________________________

______________________________

______________________________

# Toiletries

## Petroleum Jelly Mentholated & Non-Mentholated

Emergency Lubricant

Use petroleum jelly as a way to minimize friction and allow smooth movement.

## Cotton Products

Filter Water

Cotton can be used in a makeshift water filter to help remove debris.

Wound Care & First Aid

Cotton can be used as a bandage, compress, or gauze.

Insulation

Keep your hands and feet warm by adding cotton products to your socks or gloves.

Start a Fire

Starting a fire with only a spark? Cotton makes a wonderful tinder.

Emergency Water Transfer

Cotton can be used to soak up and transfer fluids from one place to another.

Makeshift Toothbrush

Use a cotton swab as an emergency makeshift toothbrush.

Makeshift Tool

A cotton swab can serve multiple purposes, such as applying substances, stirring liquids, cleaning surfaces, or even writing.

Candle Wick

Use a cotton swab with a non-plastic stick as a wick for a makeshift candle.

## Petroleum Jelly Mentholated & Non-Mentholated

Insulation

Apply petroleum jelly to your skin and dress in layered warm clothing to help insulate your body and retain heat.

Waterproofing

Petroleum can serve as a method for waterproofing various items.

Start a Fire

Petroleum jelly can be used to easily start a fire.

Prevent Rusting

Petroleum jelly can help prevent rusting by forming a moisture-resistant layer around the item.

Wound Care $ Bug Bites

Applying petroleum jelly to damaged skin creates a barrier film that helps prevent infection.

Skin & Lip Protectant

Petroleum jelly can help protect lips and skin from itching, dryness, blistering, chafing, sunburn, and chapping.

Survival Candle

Petroleum jelly can be used as the fuel for a makeshift candle. Just add a wick.

Respiratory Aid

Inhale mentholated jelly to help with cough and respiratory discomfort.

Treat Fungus Outbreak

Mentholated jelly is commonly used to treat fungus and candida.

Treat Headaches & Earaches

Mentholated jelly can reduce the perception of pain with ear, head, and muscle aches. (topical uses only)

# Toiletries

## Other Uses

______________________________

______________________________

______________________________

______________________________

## Other Uses

______________________________

______________________________

______________________________

______________________________

## Mouthwash

**Hygiene**
In emergencies, mouthwash can be used to help control body odors and maintain some sort of cleanliness.

**Bug Repellent & Bite Treatment**
The peppermint in mouthwash can be used to help ward off bugs and soothe bites.

**Makeshift Cleaner**
Mouthwash can be used to make an improvised surface cleaner. However, it may not be considered as a disinfectant due to the low level of alcohol content found in most mouthwashes.

## Razor

**Clean Fish**
Use the blades of a razor to scrape the scales off of fish.

**Makeshift Knife**
Take the blades out of the mount of a razor and use them as makeshift knives.

**Start a Fire**
Use the blades of a razor as a striker to create a spark when used with flint or a ferro rod.

**Weapon***
Use the blades as a way to create makeshift arrowheads for a spear or bow.

## Other Uses

______________________________

______________________________

______________________________

______________________________

## Other Uses

______________________________

______________________________

______________________________

______________________________

# Toiletries

## Toothpaste

**Pest Control**
Utilize the mint and calcium found in toothpaste to help keep pests away.

**Stain Remover**
Use toothpaste to help remove stains and whiten clothing.

**Remove Gum from Hair**
Toothpaste can help remove gum from your hair.

**Mask Bad Odors**
Using toothpaste is an effective way to help mask unpleasant odors such as skunk spray.

**Polish & Buff Scratches**
Use toothpaste to repair and buff damaged surfaces.

**Emergency Hair Gel**
Need a quick fix for taming those unruly flyaways? Use toothpaste as an emergency hair gel.

**Emergency Spackle**
Use toothpaste to fill, patch, and repair small holes in various surfaces.

**Surface Defogger**
Toothpaste produces a film on the surface of glasses, mirrors, or goggles that prevents fogging.

**Nail Polish Remover**
To help remove nail polish, you can mix toothpaste with citrus and use it to scrub your nails.

## Hand Sanitizer

**Start a Fire**
The isopropyl alcohol present in hand sanitizers can be used as an effective fire starter.

**Clean, Disinfect, & Sanitize**
Use hand sanitizer to clean and sanitize skin, surfaces, and materials.

**Degreaser**
Use hand sanitizer to help get rid of grease residue on skin and surfaces.

**Adhesive Removal**
Hand sanitizer can be helpful when removing sticky items.

**Topical Uses**
Hand sanitizer relieves itchy bites, eases muscle aches, and is an astringent, antiseptic, and deodorant.

**Pest Removal**
Insects hate isopropyl alcohol. Use hand sanitizer to get rid of bugs, including ants, roaches, ticks, etc.

**Defroster**
The alcohol in hand sanitizer does not freeze and can be used to help defrost a mirror or window.

## Other Uses

______________________________

______________________________

______________________________

______________________________

# Toiletries

## Eye Care Products

First Aid

100% saline without other additives can be used to flush a wound.

Pest Killer

Boric Acid found in contact lens solution can be used to help get rid of pests like ants and roaches.

Homemade Slime

Combine glue, baking soda, and contact lens solution together to make slime. You can use the slime as a way to clean debris and reduce stress.

## Moist Towelettes

Start a Fire

Utilize dried wipes crafted from organic fibers as a practical and effective material for starting fires.

Hygiene

When necessary, use moist towelettes to clean yourself from head to toe.

Clean Surfaces & Utensils

Transform ordinary wipes into germ-fighting wipes by adding alcohol to them. Then, use them to disinfect surfaces and items.

Dust Cloths

Dried wipes can be repurposed and used as improvised dusting cloths.

Storage

You can repurpose wipe containers to store various items.

Cool Down

On a hot day, use moist towelettes to help you cool down.

## Soap

Stop Poison Ivy from Spreading

It is advisable to wash the affected area with soap and water to help prevent the poison ivy extracts from spreading.

Repel & Kill Bugs

Get rid of bugs by spraying them with a solution of soapy water.

Multi-Purpose Cleaner

Make a multi-purpose cleaner by adding soap and water to a spray bottle.

Degreaser

Use soapy water to help get rid of grease and oil residue.

## Toothbrush

Spot Cleaning

Use a toothbrush to clean hard-to-reach areas.

Makeshift Knife

Sharpen the end of a toothbrush and use it as a makeshift knife.

Hair Brush

Use a toothbrush to tame flyaways.

## Other Uses

______________________________

______________________________

______________________________

______________________________

# Beauty

## Acetone

### Adhesive Removal
Acetone dissolves the bonds of adhesives such as instant glues and rubber cement.

### Start a Fire
Acetone is highly flammable and can easily start a fire.

### Stain Remover
Acetone can be used to lift unwanted paint, marker, or ink stains.

### Sanitizes Instruments & Surfaces
The antimicrobial properties of acetone can be used to sanitize surfaces. (Not for topical use!)

### Degreaser
Acetone can be used as an effective degreaser.

### Dissolves Plastic & Rubber
Extended contact with acetone can lead to the dissolution of plastic and rubber materials.

### Make "Glue" or Pseudo Plastic Material
When 100% acetone is mixed with foam, it melts and can be transformed into an improvised "glue" or plastic-like substance, depending on the ratio of acetone to foam.

## Nail Polish

### Waterproof Matches
Make waterproof matches by applying nail polish to both the match head and the wooden splint.

### Sealant/Glue
Use nail polish as a method to bond or seal torn or cracked materials.

### Start a Fire
Nail polish is a combustible material and can be utilized to start a fire.

### Secure Screws
Enhance the longevity of screws by applying nail polish to reduce thread wear.

### Tarnish & Rust-Proofing
Prevent rust formation by coating metal surfaces with nail polish.

### Fix Broken Fingernails
Use nail polish to strengthen a broken fingernail.

### Remove Warts
Applying nail polish directly to a wart is believed, but not proven, to deprive it of oxygen, potentially hindering its growth.

## Other Uses

________________________________

________________________________

________________________________

________________________________

## Other Uses

________________________________

________________________________

________________________________

________________________________

# Beauty

## Other Uses

________________________________

________________________________

________________________________

________________________________

## Hair Pin

Emergency Needle

Use a hairpin as a substitute needle for threading burlap, wool, or yarn material.

Tube Squeezer

Attach a hairpin to the end of a tube and gently squeeze upward to dispense the contents from the tube.

Improvised Zipper Tab

Utilize a hairpin as a makeshift solution to repair a broken zipper pull tab.

Fishing Hook

Shape a hairpin to resemble a fishing hook, sharpen the tip, and use it as an improvised fishing hook.

Improvised Nose Plug

Utilize a hairpin to temporarily close your nostrils in a time of need.

Lock Pick

Utilize a hairpin as an improvised lock pick. (Persistence may be required, but keep trying until successful.)

Emergency Screwdriver

Use a hairpin as an emergency screwdriver when needed.

## Hair Tie/ Rubber Band

Tourniquet Aid

Use a hair tie or rubber band to assist when tying a tourniquet by securing an improvised windlass in place. Tourniquets are used to help stop blood loss from a laceration or open wound. (Prior experience with tourniquets is advised.)

Slingshot*

A hair tie or rubber band can be used as makeshift slingshot elastic bands.

Makeshift Eraser

Use a rubber band as a makeshift eraser to effectively remove pencil markings.

Remove Screws

Place a rubber band over a stripped screw and press down firmly with a screwdriver to help loosen it.

Build a Trap

Use rubber bands to trigger an animal trap when it is encountered.

## Other Uses

________________________________

________________________________

________________________________

________________________________

# Beauty

## Other Uses

______________________________

______________________________

______________________________

______________________________

## Hair Gel

Emergency Sealant

Hair gel can temporarily seal a tear or patch a hole.

Emergency Glue

Hair gel can be used as a makeshift "glue" for soft materials that won't be subjected to tension or pulling.

## Nail Clippers

Makeshift Scissors

Nail clippers can be used as improvised shears for cutting through materials such as paper, string, or aluminium.

Can Opener

Leverage the attached nail file to make a small hole in a can. Then, use the nail clippers to cut away the remaining portion of the can.

Start a Fire

Use the attached nail file as a striker to create a spark when used with flint or a ferro rod.

## Hair Spray/ Oil Sheen

Start a Fire

Oil-based hair products are typically flammable. Spray the contents out of the can before igniting a flame to avoid unwanted explosions.

Lubricant

Use hair oil as a way to minimize friction and allow smooth movement.

Static Eliminator

Apply hairspray to fabric to eliminate static electricity.

Sealant

Apply hairspray as a method to seal and extend the lifespan of items such as tents, sleeping bags, shoes, text on paper, plant clippings, pantyhose, etc.

Adhesive Remover

Apply hairspray to aid in the removal of label stickers from products.

## Other Uses

______________________________

______________________________

______________________________

______________________________

# Beauty

## Nail File

### Sharpener

To get a precise point on items such as pencils or sticks, try using a nail file to hone the tips.

### Start a Fire

To start a fire, use a metal nail file to strike a piece of flint or a ferro rod. You can also ignite a match with an emery board or a metal nail file.

### Sanding Tool

A nail file can be used as a sanding tool to smooth surfaces and prevent splintering or rusting.

### Kitchen Utensil

A metal nail file can be used as a makeshift skewer for cooking over an open flame or as an unconventional eating utensil.

### Makeshift Knife

With a rock and a metal nail file, you can craft a makeshift knife by honing the file against the rock.

## Makeup

### Start a Fire

Certain chemicals found in makeup, such as paraffin wax, are combustible and can be helpful when starting a fire.

### Mark Your Trail

Colorful makeup can be used to display visible markers along your path when navigating through an unfamiliar area.

### Conceal Items

Conceal a small item, such as money, underneath a bandage on your skin. Apply flesh-colored makeup to help disguise the bandage, creating a discreet mini compartment that you can carry with you throughout the day.

### Sun Screen

Makeup often includes added sunscreen for enhanced protection. Utilize it when necessary for an extra layer of sun protection.

### Writing Utensil

Eyeliner and lipsticks, among other makeup items, can serve as unconventional writing instruments.

## Other Uses

______________________________

______________________________

______________________________

______________________________

## Other Uses

______________________________

______________________________

______________________________

______________________________

# Beauty

## Other Uses

______________________________

______________________________

______________________________

______________________________

## Mirror

Start a Fire

Use a mirror to focus the sun's rays and ignite tinder.

Weapon *

Channel the sun's rays through a mirror to project a beam of light into the eyes of anyone or anything posing a threat to you.

Eyes In The Back Of Your Head

Use a mirror as a tool to attain a complete 360-degree view of your surroundings.

Makeshift Knife

Utilize the sharp edges of a mirror or break it to craft a pointed edge, transforming it into an improvised knife.

## Comb & Brush

Makeshift Hammer

Use the back of a sturdy brush as an improvised hammer.

Measurement Aid

The gaps between the teeth of a comb can serve as a guide to ensure precise measurements.

## Lip Balm

Insect Control

Lip balm made with ingredients such as peppermint oil can serve as a bug repellent or provide relief for insect bites.

Survival Candle

Lip balm can be used as the fuel for a makeshift candle. Just add a wick!

Prevent Rusting

Lip balm can be used to effectively prevent rusting and tarnishing.

Emergency Lubricant

Use lip balm as a way to minimize friction and allow smooth movement.

Waterproofing

Improve the moisture resistance of items by using lip balm as a waterproofing method.

Skin Protectant

Many commercial lip balms are made with petroleum and can help alleviate dry skin, stop bleeding, prevent blistering, serve as emergency wound care, and even act as a sunscreen.

## Other Uses

______________________________

______________________________

______________________________

______________________________

# Medical Supplies

## Hydrogen Peroxide

### The Truth About H2O2 & Purifying Water

Hydrogen peroxide is an oxidizing agent and is used for dechlorination. It is a weak antimicrobial and is not approved as a standalone treatment.

### Sanitize Instruments & Surfaces

Leverage the limited antimicrobial properties of hydrogen peroxide for sanitization, whether applied topically or on surfaces.

### Oral Care

Hydrogen peroxide can be utilized to whiten teeth, alleviate a sore throat through gargling, and aid in treating canker sores and gum inflammation. (Caution: may cause intestinal pain and bleeding if swallowed.)

### Disinfect Fruits & Vegetables

Peroxide can assist in eliminating germs and the presence of pesticide residue on produce.

### Garden Aid

Diluted hydrogen peroxide can be applied to support healthy plant and seed growth.

### Treat Ear Problems

Hydrogen peroxide helps treat ear issues such as wax build-up, swimmer's ear, and ear infections.

### Kill Mold, Mildew, & Fungus

Use peroxide to stop the growth of mold, mildew, and fungus.

## Rubbing Alcohol

### Start a Fire

Isopropyl alcohol is a great fire starter.

### Clean, Disinfect, & Sanitize

Use isopropyl alcohol to clean and sanitize skin, surfaces, and materials.

### Degreaser

Use rubbing alcohol to get rid of grease residue on skin and surfaces.

### Adhesive Removal

Apply alcohol to assist in removing sticky substances.

### Topical Uses

Alcohol relieves itchy bites, eases fungal infections, helps prevent skin infections, relieves muscle aches, and is an astringent, antiseptic, and deodorant.

### Pest Removal

Insects hate isopropyl alcohol. Use it to help get rid of bugs, including ants and roaches.

### Defroster

Alcohol does not freeze and can be used to easily defrost a mirror or window.

## Other Uses

____________________

____________________

____________________

____________________

# Medical Supplies

## Aspirin

### Health Benefits

Aspirin enhances cancer survival rates, alleviates minor aches and pains, acts as an anti-inflammatory, reduces fevers, and contributes to preventing heart attacks and strokes.

### Treat a Toothache

According to experts, there is no evidence to suggest that placing a crushed aspirin pill directly on a tooth will alleviate the pain. It is recommended to take aspirin orally for pain relief.

### Garden Aid

The salicylic acid present in aspirin can help plants combat infections.

### Power a Car Battery

Aspirin undergoes a chemical decomposition process, producing acetic acid. Supposedly, when aspirin reacts with the sulfuric acid in the battery, it generates enough electrical charge to start the engine. Disclaimer: Expand your understanding and research new information that you are unsure about before attempting.

### Skin Care

Create a paste by mixing a crushed aspirin tablet with water and applying it to warts, dandruff, and calluses as a remedy for these conditions.

### Spackle

Prepare a paste by combining crushed aspirin with water and use it to mend or patch up holes.

## Condom

### Water Collection & Transfer

Condoms can be used to collect, store, and transfer water.

### Start a Fire

Fill a condom with water and focus sunlight onto tinder to initiate a fire.

### Waterproofing

Protect your items from water damage by using a condom as a protective barrier.

### Emergency Sterile Gloves

Condoms can serve as a sterile alternative to gloves for various tasks.

### First Aid

In emergency situations, a condom can function as a protective barrier for open wounds.

### Floatation Device

Inflate a condom to capacity and utilize it as a flotation device or fishing bobber.

### Makeshift Weapon*

Create a slingshot by attaching a condom to a sturdy, branched stick.

## Other Uses

_______________________________

_______________________________

_______________________________

_______________________________

# Medical Supplies

## Other Uses

______________________________

______________________________

______________________________

______________________________

## Adhesive Bandage

Emergency Tape

An adhesive bandage can act as an improvised substitute for tape.

Start a Fire

The absorbent pad in an adhesive bandage is often crafted from cotton, which is highly flammable and can be ignited with just a spark.

Storage

When not being used to cover a wound, you can store small items underneath an adhesive bandage.

## Inhaler

Water Uses

Use the actuator as a funnel, straw, or spout to direct fluids.

Start a Fire

Fill a translucent inhaler spacer with water and focus sunlight onto tinder to initiate a fire.

WARNING:

Inhaler canisters are subjected to intense pressure and could potentially explode if exposed to excessive heat.

## Pregnancy Test

Help Detect Health Ailments

A false positive pregnancy test reading could detect underlying conditions such as urinary tract infections, kidney disease (blood in urine), ovarian cancer, or pituitary problems. In circumstances where professional medical care is unavailable, a pregnancy test could be employed as a potential tool to help monitor your health status.

## Face Mask

Filter Water

Use a face mask, particularly one with an activated carbon insert, to filter water from debris.

Improvised Glue

Disposable face masks are commonly made from polypropylene (plastic). Melt it down using eco-friendly methods and use the goo to adhere items together.

Improvised Tools

You can repurpose the string or nose clip from a face mask as an improvised tool for fastening items, similar to a rubber band or bread twist tie.

## Other Uses

______________________________

______________________________

______________________________

______________________________

# Medical Supplies

## Supplements

### Start a Fire

Supplements blended with oil, such as gel fish oil capsules, can serve as fuel for a fire.

### Catch Your Next Meal

Fish oil has many uses, including attracting fish to fishing lures, enticing game animals, or masking your scent while hunting.

### Improve Mood

Maintaining a positive attitude in a survival situation is crucial, and supplements like Ashwagandha, rhodiola, passionflower, and lavender can contribute to mitigating the stress response.

### Vitamins & Minerals

In the absence of macronutrients (fats, carbs, and protein), micronutrients can be helpful but not a substitute during prolonged periods of starvation. The essential vitamins include: vitamin A, B complex, choline, C, D, E, and K. The minerals include: calcium, chloride, chromium, copper, iodine, iron, fluoride, magnesium, manganese, molybdenum, phosphorus, potassium, selenium, sodium, sulfur, and zinc. Together, they play a vital role in supporting overall health during such conditions.

### Vitamin C

Ascorbic acid cleans surfaces, preserves food, and eliminates lime and rust stains. When applied topically, it is recognized for its anti-aging, anti-pigmentary, and photoprotective properties.

## Witch Hazel

### Topical Uses:

- First aid
- Relieves hives
- Repels bugs
- Has hemostatic properties
- Soothes bug bites
- Relieves rashes
- Relieves sore muscles
- Treats acne
- Treats skin conditions
- Heals bruises faster
- Rids dandruff
- Soothes diaper rash
- Helps treat hemorrhoids
- Helps soothe eczema
- Anti-inflammatory
- Removes makeup
- Facial toner
- Vasoconstrictor
- Treats sunburn and other minor burns
- Provides vaginal care
- Treats scalp issues
- Reduces skin irritation
- Protects against skin damage
- Treats under eye bags

### Soothes Sore Throat

Bring one teaspoon of witch hazel bark to a boil in one cup of water. Gargling with this mixture may offer relief. Note: witch hazel is not used for consumption.

### Multipurpose Cleaner

Apply witch hazel as a surface cleaner, effectively removing blood stains, eliminating sticker adhesive, and serving as a mild degreaser.

# Office Supplies

## Ink Pen

### Emergency Straw

Use the barrel of a ballpoint pen as a way to drink or siphon fluids from hard-to-reach places.

### Makeshift Whistle

Make a whistle using the barrel of a pen or simply blow in the cap of certain pen brands to create a loud whistling noise.

### Makeshift Syringe

In an emergency situation, you can make an improvised syringe by using the barrel of a pen.

### Makeshift Blowgun*

Use the barrel of a pen as the chamber of a makeshift blowgun.

### Concealed Container

Store important papers or money in the barrel of a pen.

### Fishing Hook

The spring apparatus of an ink pen can easily be fashioned into a makeshift fishing hook.

### Trajectory Marker

You can determine the trajectory of a shooter by inserting a pen into a bullet hole.

### Morse Code

Click or tap a pen to communicate in Morse code.

## Pencil

### First Aid

Use a pencil to help secure a fractured finger or as an improvised windlass to tighten a tourniquet.

### Filter Fresh Water

Create a basic water filtration system and enhance its effectiveness by incorporating a layer of crushed pencil graphite into the assembly. (Note: Please do additional research on how to filter salt water using graphite.)

### Start a Fire

Use pencil shavings to help start a fire. Alternatively, you can split a pencil in half lengthwise to reveal the inner graphite layer. Then, start a fire by connecting jumper cables from a car battery to the exposed graphite. (Caution is advised.)

### Sharpen Sticks & Shave Wood

Use a pencil sharpener to sharpen sticks and create tinder from the wood shavings.

### Extend Battery Life

Rubbing a pencil eraser on the terminals of rechargeable batteries can help extend their lifespan and improve battery life.

## Other Uses

______________________________

______________________________

______________________________

______________________________

# Office Supplies



## Other Uses

________________________________

________________________________

________________________________

________________________________

## Paper

### Start a Fire

When it comes to starting a fire, paper is a clear go-to material.

### Insulation

Newspaper can be used as insulation by crumpling it up and placing it inside clothing to help stay warm.

### Toilet Paper

When all else fails, you can always use paper as improvised toilet paper.

### Draught-Proofing

Reduce unwanted air leakage in your shelter by using paper to temporarily repair gaps and prevent drafts from entering your space.

## Scissors

### Start a Fire

Create a spark by striking a piece of flint or a ferro rod.

### Makeshift Knife

Use the blade of a pair of scissors as a makeshift knife.

### Emergency Shovel

Scissors are durable and can be used to dig in tough terrain.

## Marker

### Mark Your Path

Use brightly colored highlighter or pen ink to display visible markers along your path when navigating through an unfamiliar area.

### Storage Container

Use the barrel and lid of a marker to store liquids or small objects.

## Crayon

### Start a Fire

The wax of a crayon is a useful fire starter, capable of producing a sustained flame.

### Waterproofing

The wax from a crayon is useful for waterproofing as it creates a protective layer that repels moisture.

### Sealant or Glue

Melted crayon wax can serve as a sealant or substitute for glue.

## Other Uses

________________________________

________________________________

________________________________

________________________________

# Office Supplies

## Paper Clip/ Safety Pin

**Splinter Removal**

Safety pins are effective tools for removing splinters.

**Restring a Drawstring**

Attach a string to a safety pin and insert the safety pin through the opening of the drawstring casing. Carefully guide the safety pin and string through until it comes out at the opposite end.

**Lock Pick**

A paper clip can be used as an emergency lockpick. It's important to note that practice is key to perfecting this skill.

**Fishing Hook**

Make a fishing hook with a paper clip by breaking the clip into one "J" hook, sharpening the hook, and creating a thread loop on the opposite end.

**Sewing Needle**

Create an improvised sewing needle by straightening a paper clip and making a threading loop.

**Flathead Screwdriver**

Use the end of a paper clip as a flathead screwdriver.

**Makeshift Safety Pin**

You can reshape a paper clip to create a makeshift safety pin.

**Compass**

Break a paper clip to its longest straight section. Scrape a magnet along the length of the paper clip in the same direction a few times to magnify it. The direction where you scraped will be considered "North".

## Correction Fluid & Tape

**Fire Uses**

The liquid in correction fluid is very flammable and can be used to start a fire when needed. It can also help waterproof a match head.

**Mark Your Path**

When walking, use correction fluid to mark your path for an easy way to map out your location.

**Writing Alternative**

Use correction fluid as a substitute for painting, writing, or coloring.

## Other Uses

_______________________________

_______________________________

_______________________________

_______________________________

_______________________________

_______________________________

_______________________________

_______________________________

_______________________________

_______________________________

_______________________________

# Office Supplies

## Other Uses

______________________________

______________________________

______________________________

## Glue

### The Truth About Wound Care

It's not recommended that you suture open wounds with non-medical instant adhesives due to the presence of other harmful ingredients.

### Make Slime

White craft glue can be used to make slime. Just combine glue, contact lens solution, and baking soda.

### Makeshift Shoes

Apply adhesive to the soles of your feet and wait for it to dry. This will create a protective barrier.

### Sealant

Instant adhesives can quickly seal, repair, and protect items.

### Window Cover

White craft glue can be painted on windows to create a frosted effect. This will provide you with some privacy.

### Stiffen Fabric

Use 1 part white craft glue and 1 part water to stiffen fabric.

### Fix Screws

Both stripped and loose screws can be fixed by applying glue. Allow it to dry before resuming work.

### Arrow Fletching

Use glue to make arrow fletching by creating solid leaf shapes on wax paper. After the glue dries, cut the leaf shape in half and create slits in the sides so that it resembles fletching.

## Adhesive Tape

### First Aid

Tape can be used for a variety of purposes in emergency situations, including indirectly covering wounds, preventing blisters, supporting fractures and sprains, making a sling, assisting with tourniqueting wounds, removing splinters, and even acting as a makeshift suture.

### Waterproofing

Using tape is an effective solution to protect valuable items from water damage.

### Patch Fabric & Other Materials

Tape is a convenient solution for repairing and patching up fabric and other materials.

### Arrow Fletching

Tape can be used to craft the fletching of makeshift arrows.

### Makeshift Cordage

Simply intertwine and twist together strips of tape to form a strong and sturdy cordage.

### Create Things

Use tape to create items such as dishware, a shelter, clothing, etc. The possibilities are endless!

### Insulation

Duct tape can serve as a helpful insulator. Get resourceful and use it to create makeshift survival blankets or clothing to help keep yourself warm.

### Restraints*

Use tape to restrain animals or people who are in need of some time out.

### Mark Your Path

Use tape to strategically mark your path when navigating new terrain.

# Baby

## Other Uses

---

---

---

---

## Other Uses

---

---

---

---

## Diaper

### Cold Pack

Use a diaper as an improvised cold pack by absorbing water and alcohol, then apply it to the affected area.

### Absorb Moisture

Disassemble a diaper and use the polymer pack to absorb the moisture accumulation in items such as bags or damp clothing.

### Flame Retardant

The polymer pearls in diapers offer exceptional heat resistance, making them suitable for fireproofing or as a protective barrier when handling hot items.

### Garden Aid

Polymer pearls from diapers can help retain moisture in garden soil.

### First Aid

A diaper can be used as an emergency bandage to cover wounds.

### Package Material

Securely place fragile items in a diaper to keep them safe during travel.

### Towel Alternative

Use a diaper as an improvised towel to clean yourself or surfaces.

### Insulation

Diapers can be used as improvised insulation to help keep you warm.

## Diaper Rash Cream

### Moisturizer

Diaper rash cream can be used as a moisturizer to relieve dry, itchy, and flaking skin.

### First Aid

Diaper rash cream made with zinc oxide can be used to help alleviate minor burns, sunburn, razor burn, chapped lips, chafing, minor cuts & scrapes, hemorrhoids, rashes, warts, and calluses.

### Emergency Sunscreen

Diaper rash cream that contains zinc oxide can be used as a sunscreen.

### Acne Treatment

Diaper rash cream that contains zinc oxide can help treat acne.

### Bug Bite Treatment

Diaper rash cream can help ease the itching of bug bites.

### Odor Eliminator

Use diaper rash cream to prevent body odor caused by sweat.

# Baby



## Baby Powder

Absorb Moisture

Baby powder minimizes moisture and increases friction and grip.

Extinguish a Fire or Grow a Flame

Depending on the flame size, how finely distributed the particles are, and how much powder is used, you can either extinguish a small flame or magnify a large fire. (Caution is advised!)

Remove Sand

Baby powder can be used to easily remove sand from your skin.

Odor Eliminator

Baby powder can help get rid of odor-causing bacteria by eliminating moisture.

Repel Ants

Apply baby powder in strategic areas in your home to deter ants by masking the pheromone trail of other ants.

Remove Grease & Oil

Use baby powder to help absorb oil or grease that has spilled on fabrics or surfaces.

## Bottle & Sippy Cup

Spill-Proof Liquid Dispensers

Sippy cups and bottles can be used as spill-proof containers to hold liquids or as slow-drip taps to dispense liquids at a controlled rate.

Liquid Measuring Cups

Sippy cups and bottles sometimes have measurement readings engraved on the side. Use them to help measure liquids in an emergency.

## Other Uses

____________________

____________________

____________________

____________________

## Pacifier

Controlled Dispenser Cap

Poke a hole in the nipple of a pacifier and use the nipple as the dispenser cap of a makeshift water filter to drip water out at a controlled rate.

## Baby Oil

Skin Insulator & Protectant

Baby oil can be applied topically to help relieve dry, itchy, and flaking skin. Also, it can help keep you warm.

Remove Paint

Can't remove the paint from your skin? Baby oil can be used to help remove the paint.

Lubricant

Use baby oil to loosen up rusted or immovable items.

Remove Adhesives & Bubblegum

Use baby oil to help remove sticky substances.

Shine Surfaces

Use baby oil to shine surfaces such as wood, metal, and leather.

# Baby

## Plush Toys

Insulation

Use plush toys as a way to help keep warm by using the stuffing as insulation.

Start a Fire

The cotton stuffing, fur, and fabric of a plush toy can easily be ignited to start a fire.

Cordage

Twist and braid the stuffing of a plush toy into emergency cordage.

Collect, Transfer, & Filter Water

Use a stuffed toy to absorb, transfer, and filter water in an emergency.

Fishing Bobber

Cut off a small portion of a stuffed animal (such as a hand) and use it as a fishing bobber.

## Baby Doll

Emergency Cordage

Snip off the baby doll's hair and braid it together piece by piece to create a long cord for emergency use.

Emergency Straw & Water Container

Hollowed-out baby doll arms and legs can be used as emergency drinking straws or containers to hold and transfer water.

Emergency Building Apparatus

Use the ball and joint hinges (arms, legs, and torso) as a way to build makeshift traps and complete other projects.

## Ball

Emergency Flotation Device

Use a ball as an emergency flotation device.

Emergency Fabric

The material used to make balls can be repurposed as an emergency fabric.

Collect Water

Cut open a ball and use it to collect water.

Storage

Cut open a ball and use it to store items whenever needed.

## Building Sets

Build Useful Things

Use building blocks to craft useful objects like cups, plates, boxes, traps, and storage containers.

Water Collection

In emergencies, singular building blocks can be used to collect and transfer water.

## Modeling Clay/Slime

Stress Reliever

Play with slime, putty, or clay during stressful situations to help elevate mood.

Spot Clean

Use slime, putty, or clay to adhere to dirt and clean areas that are too hard to reach.

Insoles For Shoes

Create makeshift insoles to alleviate sore feet.

Wall Putty

Use slime to patch holes or as an adhesive to hang lightweight items.

# Tools



## Lighter

Makeshift Solder

Create a makeshift soldering tool by attaching a blade above the flame or wrapping a metal wire around a lighter, positioning one end over the flame to heat up like a soldering iron.

Space Saver

Store tape, wire, or cord around a lighter for convenient access to these materials when required.

Create Fire Without Lighter Fuel

Start a fire by igniting tinder, such as cotton, with sparks from a lighter that does not contain lighter fluid.

## Matches

Waterproof Your Matches

Enhance the longevity of matches and make them waterproof by applying substances like wax, petroleum jelly, nail polish, or oil.

Projectile*

You can employ matches as projectiles by flicking them or launching them with a rubber band.

## Plastic Bag

Start a Fire

Initiate a fire with tinder by filling a transparent plastic bag with water and harnessing the sun's rays.

Collect Water

Utilize a plastic bag to generate water through condensation from non-toxic leaves or other damp materials. Additionally, it serves as a means to transport water.

Wound Care

A clean, unused bag can be used to dress a wound in an emergency.

Makeshift Gloves

A bag offers a convenient solution to avoid touching surfaces directly with your bare hands.

Gardening Aid

A bag can serve as a conducive environment for the growth of seedlings and mushroom spores by maintaining humidity.

Waterproofing

Protect your belongings from water damage by using a plastic bag.

## Other Uses

______________________________

______________________________

______________________________

______________________________

# Tools

## Keys/Key Ring

Makeshift Screwdriver

A key can be used to turn a screw if needed.

Lock Pick

Old keys can be modified, and key rings can be reshaped and used to gain access to locked areas. (Persistence may be required, but keep trying until successful.)

Pop A Bottle Cap

With a little bit of effort, a key can be used to remove the cap from a glass bottle.

## Flashlight

Morse Code

Use a flashlight to signal for help or communicate using Morse Code.

Space Saver

Wrap tape, wire, or cordage around a flashlight to store it for later use. Carrying a light load while traveling on foot is extremely important.

Break a Window

Use a flashlight as a window breaker when needed.

Self-Defense*

Use the beam of light to disorient your attacker and the flashlight itself as a makeshift melee weapon.

## Eating Utensils

Reflective Surface

In an emergency, a piece of silverware can be used as a reflective surface to mirror the sun's rays to indicate distress or ignite a fire.

Makeshift Shovel

Use utensils as a way to displace dirt and dig a hole.

## Multitool

Multi Uses

A multi-tool serves various purposes. Presented below is a compilation of verbs outlining the diverse functions a multi-tool can perform. Feel free to utilize this list for any other tool not explicitly mentioned in this guide. Common applications for a multitool encompass: sculpting, carving, slicing, opening, extracting, securing, leveraging, honing, impacting, smoothing, hammering, peeling, sawing, fastening, and more.

## Other Uses

______________________________

______________________________

______________________________

______________________________

# Tools

## Coins

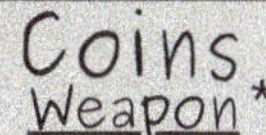

### Weapon*

Fill a sock with coins and use it as a melee weapon.

### Hot/Cold Pack

Fill a sock with coins, put it in the freezer or dip it in cold water, and use it as a makeshift cold pack. Alternatively, heat the coins and use them as a heating pad.

### Hardware Uses

A coin can be used as a makeshift screwdriver, or you can make a metal washer by drilling a hole into a coin.

### Check Tire Thread

With the head facing down, place a penny in the treads of a tire. It is believed that if the thread extends past the head of the president, then the tires are still good.

### Garden Uses (Old Gardener's Trick)

Pennies are added to soil to extend plant freshness, repel garden slugs, and act as a natural fungicide.

### Health Care & the Truth About Copper Jewelry Treating Arthritis

Pennies made before 1982 and weigh 3.11 grams are made of 95% copper and can be made into a drinking cup for its antimicrobial properties. There is no evidence that copper jewelry treats arthritis. (Beware of rusting.)

## Phone Charger

### Emergency Cordage

Use a charger cord as emergency rope.

### Makeshift Tool*

Repurpose a phone charger cord and wall block as versatile tools that can be used for anchoring, hammering, or even as a swinging weapon.

## Technology

### Repurposing

Technological devices can be reused and repurposed for many projects requiring electrical components.

### Deconstruction

Use pieces such as glass or metal bits to build or repair things for other projects.

### Signal For Help

Use reflective screens to reflect the sun's rays to signal for help.

## Smokables

### Old Remedies that Used 100% Tobacco

Tobacco leaves were once used to alleviate pain, relieve constipation, alleviate earache, ease headaches, induce vomiting (emetic), as a poultice for wounds, burns, and poisonous bites. Caution: these methods were practiced until the end of the 16th century and are no longer implemented or tenable.

### Start a Fire

Use the contents of a cigarette to help start a fire.

### Filter Water

Use cigarette filters as the bottom layer in a makeshift water filter to help remove debris.

### Pest Control

Steep tobacco in boiling water to create a natural pesticide, add to a bottle, and spray areas where pests hang out. Caution: Avoid gardens with useful plants because it may be harmful to them.

# Clothing

## Bra

### Face Mask

Place a bra cup over your nose and mouth and use it as a face mask in times of need.

### Wearable Storage

Hide items in your bra, such as money, keys, or other important items.

### Lock Pick

Use the underwire in a bra to pick a lock. (Persistence may be required, but keep trying until successful.)

## Umbrella

### Catch Emergency Rainwater

An umbrella can be used to catch rainwater by flipping it upside-down to collect or funnel the water into a bucket.

### Fabric

The fabric from an umbrella can serve many purposes, such as making improvised clothing.

### Shelter

An umbrella can be used as the roof of a small makeshift shelter.

## Panties

### Concealed Hideaway

Hide small items in the gusset or the open pocket located in the crotch area of panties.

### Elastic Band Uses*

The elastic band in underwear can be repurposed to make items such as a slingshot or a garter holster.

## Other Uses

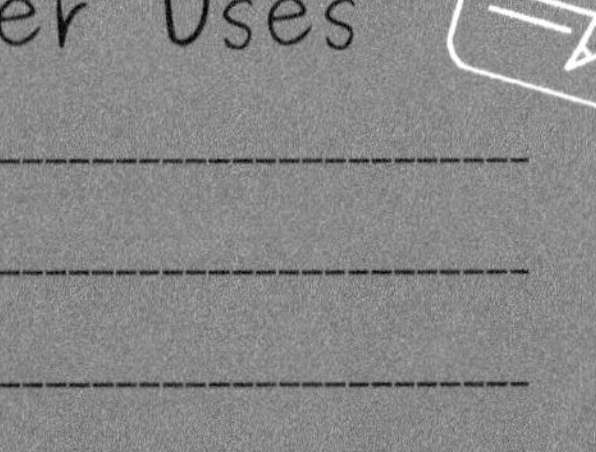

______________________________

______________________________

______________________________

______________________________

## Pantyhose

### Strainer

Use pantyhose to strain liquids in the same way you would use a cheesecloth.

### Mosquito Net

Pantyhose can serve as an improvised mosquito net to protect you from insect bites.

### Fishing Net

Pantyhose can be used to catch fish and other animals like crawfish, turtles, or even crabs.

### Face Mask

Use pantyhose as a face mask for improved air filtration.

### Water Filter

Create a makeshift straining system by using pantyhose to filter water.

### First Aid

Pantyhose can be a versatile tool for first aid. They can be used as a sling for fractured limbs, a compress for open wounds, and even as an improvised tourniquet.

# Clothing

## Other Fabric & Clothing

### Char Cloth

Char cloth can be made by placing fabric in an enclosed fire-resistant container, like a candy tin with small holes poked in it. Heat the container until the contents are black and smooth before it starts to crumble. This specially crafted material is used as tinder to ignite a fire with just a spark.

### First Aid

Use fabric as a sling for fractured limbs, a compress for open wounds, or as an improvised tourniquet.

### Collect & Filter Water

Use fabric to make a temporary straining system for collecting and filtering water.

### Face Mask

Protect your face from wind and dust by creating a simple fabric face mask.

### Mark Your Path

Strategically place ripped fabric to mark your path when navigating new terrain.

### Trap

Use fabrics in a makeshift trap to capture fish or small animals.

### Storage

Create a carrying bag from fabric to store extra items.

### Wind Direction & Smoke Signaling

Use fabric to track the direction of the wind or to make smoke signals to message for help.

### Restraints*

Use fabric to restrain animals or people who are in need of some time out.

## Glasses

### Start a Fire

Focus sunlight through the lenses of glasses to heat tinder and ignite a fire.

### Signal for Help

Reflect the sun's rays to signal for help.

### Protection

Use eyewear to protect your eyes from the elements and flying debris.

### Hinge Uses

Use the hinges of eyewear to complete projects such as constructing the door hinges for an improvised survival shelter.

### Makeshift Knife

Sharpen the lenses of eyewear and use them as makeshift blades.

## Jewelry

### Etch & Cut Glass or Metal

Diamonds can be used to scratch or cut glass and metal.

### Makeshift Pin

Use earrings as a makeshift thumb tack, safety pin, or hammering nail.

## Other Uses

______________________________

______________________________

______________________________

______________________________

# Clothing

## Hat

Wearable Storage

Use a hat to conceal and carry your personal items while you're on the go. It's a discreet and convenient way to keep your belongings within reach and out of sight.

Makeshift Trap

Use a hat as an improvised trap to catch fish and small animals.

Complete Projects

Use the snapback straps or fasteners of a hat when completing a project that requires a closure piece.

Shovel

Use the bill of a cap to shovel softened dirt, clay, or sand.

Filter Water

If the hat is constructed from a porous material, it can be used as an impromptu filter to remove harmful debris from water.

## Other Uses

________________________________

________________________________

________________________________

________________________________

________________________________

________________________________

________________________________

________________________________

## Other Uses

________________________________

________________________________

________________________________

________________________________

## Shoes

Fishing Line

Shoe strings can be used as an emergency fishing line.

Bowstring

Use a shoestring as a bowstring.

Start a Fire

Organic fabrics like cotton, commonly used in shoemaking, possess flammable properties and can be utilized to start a fire.

Makeshift Trap

Use a shoestring to make a snare trap or place bait in the shoe to lure small animals into a trap.

Escape from Zipper Tie Hand Cuffs

Fasten your shoelaces in a knot around the zipper tie while your shoes are still on. Generate friction by pedaling your legs to loosen and break the tie.

Complete Projects

Deconstruct a shoe and use its components to complete different projects.

# Other Items

# Other Items

# Other Items

# Other Items

# Helpful Tips

## Uncommon Flammable Materials

Nuts/Seeds (oil)
100% Extracts (vanilla, etc.)
Citrus Peels (oil/dried)
Sugar (molten)
Medications (added alcohol)
Moth Balls (dangerous!)

Powdered Food (finely distributed particles such as flour, etc.)
Pine Tree Resin
Ping Pong Balls (creates an intense smoke when ignited)

## Common Edible Bugs**

Ants
Grasshoppers
Earthworms
Termites
Dragonflies
Stink Bugs
Cicadas
Crickets
Meal Worms
Grubs

## What Bugs to Avoid

Snails & Slugs
Uncooked Bugs
ALL Brightly Colored Bugs
If Allergic to Shellfish
If Uncertain About Bug Species

## Fire Safety

When building a fire, it's important to create a well-ventilated area to avoid competing with the flames for oxygen. Remember, fire needs to breathe.

## Plastic Uses

Items that are made with plastic can be melted down and repurposed to create new items or can be used as an improvised sealant or glue.

Safe ways to melt plastic:

- Heat Gun
- Acetone
- Oven

## Consideration of Weight

Please be aware of the number of items that you carry on your person. The weight of your gear accumulates quickly, leading to decreased speed and efficiency.

## There is No Such Thing as Trash

Resources are important no matter how useless they may appear at first glance.

## Filtration vs Purification

Filtration involves separating solid matter from water using a filter, allowing only fluid to pass through. Purification is a process that removes impurities such as waterborne protozoa, bacteria, microorganisms, and viruses through various techniques such as boiling, disinfection, chlorination, distillation, UV radiation, or reverse osmosis.

Larger Rocks
Small Rocks
Charcoal
Charcoal Powder
Sand
Cotton/Fabric

Water Filter

149°

Purify

WARNING: Burning plastic is illegal and extremely harmful to the environment and human health.

# Helpful Tips

## The Easiest Edible Plants to Identify** in North America
(Right in your back yard)

**Dandelion**

Edible Parts:
The entire plant, from roots, leaves, and flowers, can be eaten.

Identifying Characteristics:
Flower: Yellow, ray-shaped clusters
Leaf: Spiked, toothed leaves

**Clover**

Edible Parts:
The entire plant, from roots, leaves, and flowers, can be eaten.

Identifying Characteristics:
Flower: white, pink, red spherical heads
Leaf: Trefoil leaves

Look-Alikes: Is it edible? (circle if the look-alikes for each plant are edible or not)

Catsear: Edible Not Edible
Sow Thistle: Edible Not Edible
Nipplewort: Edible Not Edible

Wood Sorrel: Edible Not Edible
Black Medic: Edible Not Edible
Shamrock: Edible Not Edible

## What Plants to Avoid

- Mushrooms (if you are not experienced)
- Areas that have been treated with pesticides and herbicides
- Bitter or soapy flavors
- White, milky sap
- Fine hairs and spines on the leaves or stems
- Waxy leaves
- Plants with a strong odor
- If animals eat it, it doesn't mean that you can!
- If you are not 100% sure, leave it alone!

## Other Common Edible** Plants that are Not Hard to Identify

- Common Berries
- Wild Onion
- Cattails
- Acorns
- Prickly Pear Cactus

Beware of Look-Alikes

**This is not an exhaustive guide, but rather a quick reference to highlight commonly found edible plants and bugs that are easily identifiable to many people in North America. It is essential to undergo professional training to become acquainted with the flora and insects in your region. Avoid handling or consuming any plant or bug if you are uncertain of its safety. Additionally, remember that some bugs and plants require specific preparation to be edible. Be cautious of potentially harmful bugs or plants that may resemble edible ones.

# Helpful Tips

## Fire Starters & Burning Materials

<u>Tinder:</u> A flammable material that ignites easily using manual fire-making techniques such as:

- Creating a spark (flint/ferro rod)
- Generating friction (literally rubbing sticks together with the assistance of a hand-operated tool such as a bow drill)
- Using compressed air (fire piston)
- Harnessing solar power (concentrating sunlight with a lens)

<u>The Best Forms of Tinder:</u>

- Natural fabric made with cotton, etc.
- Dryer lint
- Dandelion & cattail fluff

<u>Other Forms of Tinder:</u>

- Wood shavings
- Crushed dry leaves and pine needles

<u>Kindling:</u> An easily combustible material used to increase the size of a flame.

- Dry twigs, branches, and split wood about the width of a pencil.

<u>Fuel:</u> A combustible material that maintains, spreads, and prolongs a fire.

- Larger dry branches, split wood, and logs.

## Common Types of Knots

<u>Figure 8 Knot</u>
Requires 1 rope or double up the same rope
<u>Uses:</u> climbing and sailing

<u>Square Knot</u>
Requires 2 separate ropes
<u>Uses:</u> first aid, securing, and binding

<u>Bowline Knot</u>
Requires 1 rope
<u>Uses:</u> hoisting, hauling, and fastening one rope to another

*<u>Makeshift Weapons Disclosure</u>

Self-defense and hunting laws can be quite unpredictable. Research the laws in your area and use decrement before attempting to booby trap, hunt, or creatively defend yourself.

# For Your Information

## Soap Making 101

<u>How Lye is Made</u>

Lye is made when the ashes from a hardwood fire and soft water are combined, boiled (for faster results), and left to sit until the pH of the solution is 11.5 or higher.

<u>CAUTION:</u> If you are considering making your own lye, it is highly recommended that you use personal protective equipment. Be sure to research the correct procedures, follow detailed instructions, and comply with legal regulations before attempting to create lye. Keep in mind that lye is a potent alkaline substance that can cause burns and other health risks if mishandled.

# How to Make Cold Process Soap 

Commercially Produced Lye: Sodium hydroxide is used to make bar soap, and potassium hydroxide is used to make liquid soap.

## Ingredients:

1. Lye
2. Water
3. Fats or oils (such as animal fats, olive oil, coconut oil, palm oil, etc.)
4. Optional: Essential oils, herbs, or other additives for fragrance and texture

## Equipment:

1. Heat-resistant containers and stirring utensils (stainless steel or silicone)
2. Thermometer
3. Scale
4. Stick blender
5. Mold for shaping the soap
6. Safety gear (gloves, goggles, long sleeves)

Important: The ratios of lye to water and fats/oils to lye/water solution can differ.

## Steps:

1. Safety Precautions:
   - Put on safety gear to protect yourself when handling lye.
2. Measure Ingredients:
   - Note: different oils/fats need different amounts of lye water solution to turn into soap. For example: A blend of 20 oz coconut oil and 10 oz olive oil can be safely mixed with 4.78 oz lye and 9 oz water solution.
   - Weigh the fats or oils using a scale.
   - Measure the lye carefully according to the directions on the packaging.
3. Melting Fats/Oils:
   - If the fats/oils are solid, gently heat the fats or oils until they are fully melted.
4. Mixing Lye Solution:
   - In a well-ventilated area, slowly add the lye to water (NEVER add water to lye). Stir until the lye is fully dissolved.
5. Cooling Fats/Oils & Lye Solution:
   - Allow the lye solution & fats/oils to cool. Both the lye solution and the fats/oils should be around 100-130°F (37-54°C) when combined.
6. Blending and Saponification:
   - Slowly pour the lye solution into the melted fats/oils. Use a stick blender to mix the ingredients until it is a thickened consistency resembling pudding. This may take several minutes.
7. Optional Additives:
   - Add essential oils, herbs, or other additives for fragrance or texture. Stir thoroughly.
8. Molding & Curing the Soap:
   - Pour the soap mixture into the soap mold. Allow the soap to cure for 24-48 hours. Afterward, cut it into bars if desired.

# Morse Code

1
• — — — —

2
• • — — —

3
• • • — —

4
• • • • —

5
• • • • •

6
— • • • •

7
— — • • •

8
— — — • •

9
— — — — •

0
— — — — —

## Communicating in Morse Code:

● "DIT" Short Tone:

It's just a quick tap of a pen, a flash of a flashlight, or a blow of a whistle.

— "DAH" Long Tone:

It's a slower, more prolonged tone about the length of 3 dits.

## Spacing Between Characters:

How to Space out the Dits & Dahs in a Single Number or Letter:

Spacing is equivalent to 1 dit

How to Space out the Numbers or Letters in a Single Word:

Spacing is equivalent to 3 dits

Spacing Between Words:

Spacing is equivalent to 7 dits

# Morse Code

A •–
B –•••
C –•–•
D –••
E •
F ••–•

G ––•
H ••••
I ••
J •–––
K –•–
L •–••

M ––
N –•
O –––
P •––•
Q ––•–

R •–•
S •••
T –
U ••–
V •••–
W •––

X –••–
Y –•––
Z ––••

SOS • • • – – – • • •

Easy Way To Remember SOS:

- 3 quick, 3 slow, 3 quick
- Use the guide below:
  - Say "shit is real" fast for "S" and "Oh my God" slow for "O" while flashing, beeping, tapping, etc...

Shit is Real Oh My God Shit Is Real

# Notes

# Notes

# Notes

# Notes

# References

The content of this book is primarily sourced from evidence-based references. Furthermore, the author's extensive study and education in the field of nutrition have also influenced the data presented. It is important to note that the information provided is not an exhaustive list of facts. Instead, readers are encouraged to use this information as a starting point for their own evidence-based research.

# References

Ajmera, R. (2018, July 16). 8 Benefits and Uses of Witch Hazel. Healthline; Healthline Media. https://www.healthline.com/nutrition/witch-hazel-benefits-uses

Ajmera, R. (2022, January 11). 9 Unique Benefits of Coffee. Healthline. https://www.healthline.com/nutrition/top-evidence-based-health-benefits-of-coffee

Ajmera, R. (2024, January 29). 10 Home Remedies to Get Rid of Dandruff Naturally. Healthline; Healthline Media. https://www.healthline.com/nutrition/ways-to-treat-dandruff

Arif H, Aggarwal S. Salicylic Acid (Aspirin) [Updated 2023 Jul 5]. In: StatPearls [Internet]. Treasure Island (FL): StatPearls Publishing; 2024 Jan-. Available from: https://www.ncbi.nlm.nih.gov/books/NBK519032/

Arif T. (2015). Salicylic acid as a peeling agent: a comprehensive review. Clinical, cosmetic and investigational dermatology, 8, 455-461. https://doi.org/10.2147/CCID.S84765

Ajmera, R., & Hill, A. (2018, July 18). Dandelion: Health Benefits and Side Effects. Healthline. https://www.healthline.com/nutrition/dandelion-benefits

Alagawany, M., Elnesr, S. S., Farag, M. R., Abd El-Hack, M. E., Khafaga, A. F., Taha, A. E., Tiwari, R., Yatoo, M. I., Bhatt, P., Marappan, G., & Dhama, K. (2019). Use of Licorice (Glycyrrhiza glabra) Herb as a Feed Additive in Poultry: Current Knowledge and Prospects. Animals : an open access journal from MDPI, 9(8), 536. https://doi.org/10.3390/ani9080536

Allahghadri, T., Rasooli, I., Owlia, P., Nadooshan, M. J., Ghazanfari, T., Taghizadeh, M., & Astaneh, S. D. (2010). Antimicrobial property, antioxidant capacity, and cytotoxicity of essential oil from cumin produced in Iran. Journal of food science, 75(2), H54-H61. https://doi.org/10.1111/j.1750-3841.2009.01467.x

Al-Niaimi, F., & Chiang, N. Y. Z. (2017). Topical Vitamin C and the Skin: Mechanisms of Action and Clinical Applications. The Journal of clinical and aesthetic dermatology, 10(7), 14-17.

Arshad, M. S., Imran, M., Ahmed, A., Sohaib, M., Ullah, A., Nisa, M. U., Hina, G., Khalid, W., & Rehana, H. (2019). Tamarind: A diet-based strategy against lifestyle maladies. Food science & nutrition, 7(11), 3378-3390. https://doi.org/10.1002/fsn3.1218

Arslan, K., Karahan, O., Okuş, A., Unlü, Y., Eryılmaz, M. A., Ay, S., & Sevinç, B. (2012). Comparison of topical zinc oxide and silver sulfadiazine in burn wounds: an experimental study. Ulusal travma ve acil cerrahi dergisi = Turkish journal of trauma & emergency surgery : TJTES, 18(5), 376-383. https://doi.org/10.5505/tjtes.2012.45381

# References


Balakrishnan, R., Azam, S., Kim, I. S., & Choi, D. K. (2023). Neuroprotective Effects of Black Pepper and Its Bioactive Compounds in Age-Related Neurological Disorders. Aging and disease, 14(3), 750-777. https://doi.org/10.14336/AD.2022.1022

Bennato, F., Ianni, A., Innosa, D., Martino, C., Grotta, L., Pomilio, F., Verna, M., & Martino, G. (2019). Influence of Licorice Root Feeding on Chemical-Nutritional Quality of Cow Milk and Stracciata Cheese, an Italian Traditional Fresh Dairy Product. Animals : an open access journal from MDPI, 9(12), 1153. https://doi.org/10.3390/ani9121153

Bode, A. M., & Dong, Z. (2011). The Amazing and Mighty Ginger. In I. F. F. Benzie (Eds.) et. al., Herbal Medicine: Biomolecular and Clinical Aspects. (2nd ed.). CRC Press/Taylor & Francis.

Burns J. (2023). Common herbs for stress: The science and strategy of a botanical medicine approach to self-care. Journal of interprofessional education & practice, 30, 100592. https://doi.org/10.1016/j.xjep.2022.100592

Butt, M. S., Pasha, I., Sultan, M. T., Randhawa, M. A., Saeed, F., & Ahmed, W. (2013). Black pepper and health claims: a comprehensive treatise. Critical reviews in food science and nutrition, 53(9), 875-886. https://doi.org/10.1080/10408398.2011.571799

Cafasso, J. (2018, July 20). Steam Inhalation: Cold, Sinuses, Procedure, Benefits, Cough, and. Healthline. https://www.healthline.com/health/steam-inhalation

Campbell-Falck, D., Thomas, T., Falck, T. M., Tutuo, N., & Clem, K. (2000). The intravenous use of coconut water. The American journal of emergency medicine, 18(1), 108-111. https://doi.org/10.1016/s0735-6757(00)90062-7

Cassell, Dana K. "Mixing Chemical and Physical Sunscreens Can Make Them Degrade." Healthline, 19 Oct. 2021, www.healthline.com/health-news/mixing-chemical-and-physical-sunscreens-can-make-them-degrade.

Center for Drug Evaluation and Research. (2019). Aspirin for Reducing Your Risk of Heart Attack and Stroke. U.S. Food and Drug Administration. https://www.fda.gov/drugs/safe-daily-use-aspirin/aspirin-reducing-your-risk-heart-attack-and-stroke-know-facts

Charles Alexis, A. (2022, February 15). Is Clover Edible? Nutrients, Benefits, and Downsides. Healthline. https://www.healthline.com/nutrition/is-clover-edible#types

Charlton A. (2004). Medicinal uses of tobacco in history. Journal of the Royal Society of Medicine, 97(6), 292-296. https://doi.org/10.1177/014107680409700614

# References


Cherney, K. (2018a, August 7). Does Coffee Have Any Benefits for Your Skin? Healthline; Healthline Media. https://www.healthline.com/health/coffee-benefits-for-skin

Cherney, K. (2018b, October 19). Witch Hazel for Face: Benefits and Risks for Skin Conditions. Healthline. https://www.healthline.com/health/witch-hazel-for-face

Deutch, M. R., Grimm, D., Wehland, M., Infanger, M., & Krüger, M. (2019). Bioactive Candy: Effects of Licorice on the Cardiovascular System. Foods (Basel, Switzerland), 8(10), 495. https://doi.org/10.3390/foods8100495

Dodds M. W. (2012). The oral health benefits of chewing gum. Journal of the Irish Dental Association, 58(5), 253-261.

Drews R. C. (1977). Acetone sterilization in ophthalmic surgery. Annals of ophthalmology, 9(6), 781-784.

Eccles R. (2000). Role of cold receptors and menthol in thirst, the drive to breathe and arousal. Appetite, 34(1), 29-35. https://doi.org/10.1006/appe.1999.0291

EPA. "Water Treatment Chemical Supply Chain Profile – Hydrogen Peroxide." EPA.gov. EPA 817-F-22-030

Fellows, J., & Crestodina, L. (2006). Home-prepared saline: a safe, cost-effective alternative for wound cleansing in home care. Journal of wound, ostomy, and continence nursing : official publication of The Wound, Ostomy and Continence Nurses Society, 33(6), 606-609. https://doi.org/10.1097/00152192-200611000-00003

Frothingham, S. (2018, August 28). Super Glue on Cuts: When and Why to Use It. Healthline. https://www.healthline.com/health/super-glue-on-cuts

Ginta, D. (2017, March 17). Everything You Need to Know About Petroleum Jelly. Healthline; Healthline Media. https://www.healthline.com/health/beauty-skin-care/petroleum-jelly

Goldman, R. (2018, September 20). 11 Effective Earache Remedies. Healthline. https://www.healthline.com/health/11-effective-earache-remedies

Gotter, A. (2017, August 17). Home Remedies for Athlete's Foot. Healthline. https://www.healthline.com/health/home-remedies-for-athletes-foot

Groninger, H., & Schisler, R. E. (2012). Topical capsaicin for neuropathic pain #255. Journal of palliative medicine, 15(8), 946-947. https://doi.org/10.1089/jpm.2012.9571

# References

Gudritz, L. (2017, August 17). Some Like It Hot: 5 Reasons Spicy Food Is Good for You. Healthline. https://www.healthline.com/health/five-reasons-to-eat-spicy-foods

Gunnars, K., & Bailey, D. (2020, April 6). 10 Evidence-Based Benefits of Green Tea. Healthline. https://www.healthline.com/nutrition/top-10-evidence-based-health-benefits-of-green-tea#The-bottom-line

Gupta, M., Mahajan, V. K., Mehta, K. S., & Chauhan, P. S. (2014). Zinc therapy in dermatology: a review. Dermatology research and practice, 2014, 709152. https://doi.org/10.1155/2014/709152

Hekmatpou, D., Mehrabi, F., Rahzani, K., & Aminiyan, A. (2019). The Effect of Aloe Vera Clinical Trials on Prevention and Healing of Skin Wound: A Systematic Review. Iranian journal of medical sciences, 44(1), 1-9.

Hetherington, M. M., & Regan, M. F. (2011). Effects of chewing gum on short-term appetite regulation in moderately restrained eaters. Appetite, 57(2), 475-482. https://doi.org/10.1016/j.appet.2011.06.008

Hubbard, A. (2021, April 7). Witch Hazel for Hair: Benefits, Recipes, and How to Use. Healthline. https://www.healthline.com/health/witch-hazel-for-hair

Hursel, R., & Westerterp-Plantenga, M. S. (2013). Catechin- and caffeine-rich teas for control of body weight in humans. The American journal of clinical nutrition, 98(6 Suppl), 1682S-1693S. https://doi.org/10.3945/ajcn.113.058396

Ikeda, A., Miyamoto, J. J., Usui, N., Taira, M., & Moriyama, K. (2018). Chewing Stimulation Reduces Appetite Ratings and Attentional Bias toward Visual Food Stimuli in Healthy-Weight Individuals. Frontiers in psychology, 9, 99. https://doi.org/10.3389/fpsyg.2018.00099

Is Taking Aspirin Good for Your Heart? (n.d.). Www.hopkinsmedicine.org. https://www.hopkinsmedicine.org/health/wellness-and-prevention/is-taking-aspirin-good-for-your-heart#:~:text=Aspirin

Kazimierska, K., & Kalinowska-Lis, U. (2021). Milk Proteins—Their Biological Activities and Use in Cosmetics and Dermatology. Molecules (Basel, Switzerland), 26(11), 3253. https://doi.org/10.3390/molecules26113253

Khan, N., & Mukhtar, H. (2013). Tea and health: studies in humans. Current pharmaceutical design, 19(34), 6141-6147. https://doi.org/10.2174/1381612811319340008

Kragh, J. F., Jr, & Dubick, M. A. (2017). Bleeding Control With Limb Tourniquet Use in the Wilderness Setting: Review of Science. Wilderness & environmental medicine, 28(2S), S25-S32. https://doi.org/10.1016/j.wem.2016.11.006

# References

Kragh, J. F., Jr, Wallum, T. E., Aden, J. K., 3rd, Dubick, M. A., & Baer, D. G. (2015). Which Improvised Tourniquet Windlasses Work Well and Which Ones Won't?. Wilderness & environmental medicine, 26(3), 401-405. https://doi.org/10.1016/j.wem.2014.12.028

Landes, E. (2020, October 14). Aloe Vera for Hair: Benefits for Hair Growth. Healthline. https://www.healthline.com/health/aloe-vera-for-hair

Lang, A. (2020, September 2). Copper Water: Basics, Benefits, and Downsides. Healthline. https://www.healthline.com/nutrition/copper-water-benefits

Lee, C., Porter, K. M., & Hodgetts, T. J. (2007). Tourniquet use in the civilian prehospital setting. Emergency medicine journal : EMJ, 24(8), 584-587. https://doi.org/10.1136/emj.2007.046359

Lee, J., Lee, E., Kim, Y., Kim, E., & Lee, Y. (2016). Effects of gum chewing on abdominal discomfort, nausea, vomiting and intake adherence to polyethylene glycol solution of patients in colonoscopy preparation. Journal of clinical nursing, 25(3-4), 518-525. https://doi.org/10.1111/jocn.13086

Leiva, C. (2021, June 10). Saltwater Rinse Benefits for Oral Health and How to Make It. Healthline. https://www.healthline.com/health/dental-and-oral-health/salt-water-rinse

Lopes, S. O., Abrantes, L. C. S., Azevedo, F. M., Morais, N. S., Morais, D. C., Gonçalves, V. S. S., Fontes, E. A. F., Franceschini, S. D. C. C., & Priore, S. E. (2023). Food Insecurity and Micronutrient Deficiency in Adults: A Systematic Review and Meta-Analysis. Nutrients, 15(5), 1074. https://doi.org/10.3390/nu15051074

Luo, S. D., Chen, W. C., Wu, C. N., Yang, Y. H., Li, S. H., Fang, F. M., Huang, T. L., Wang, Y. M., Chiu, T. J., & Wu, S. C. (2020). Low-Dose Aspirin Use Significantly Improves the Survival of Late-stage NPC: A Propensity Score-Matched Cohort Study in Taiwan. Cancers, 12(6), 1551. https://doi.org/10.3390/cancers12061551

Madreseh-Ghahfarokhi, S., Pirali, Y., Dehghani-Samani, A., & Dehghani-Samani, A. (2018). The insecticidal and repellent activity of ginger (Zingiber officinale) and eucalyptus (Eucalyptus globulus) essential oils against Culex theileri Theobald, 1903 (Diptera: Culicidae. Annals of parasitology, 64(4), 351-360. https://doi.org/10.17420/ap6404.171

Mahdizadeh, S., Sawford, K., van Andel, M., & Browning, G. F. (2020). Efficacy of citric acid and sodium hypochlorite as disinfectants against Mycoplasma bovis. Veterinary microbiology, 243, 108630. https://doi.org/10.1016/j.vetmic.2020.108630

# References


Marshall, M. V., Cancro, L. P., & Fischman, S. L. (1995). Hydrogen peroxide: a review of its use in dentistry. Journal of periodontology, 66(9), 786-796. https://doi.org/10.1902/jop.1995.66.9.786

McGrane, K. (2020, June 12). Licorice Root: Benefits, Uses, Precautions, and Dosage. Healthline. https://www.healthline.com/nutrition/licorice-root

Minh, V. N., Yen, V. H., Hoa, D. T., Huong, N. T., & Hao, B. Q. (2023). Effectiveness and safety of a cream product containing zinc oxide for alleviating mosquito bite symptoms. Cutaneous and ocular toxicology, 42(4), 209-212. https://doi.org/10.1080/15569527.2023.2234030

Mohd Sabee, M. M. S., Itam, Z., Beddu, S., Zahari, N. M., Mohd Kamal, N. L., Mohamad, D., Zulkepli, N. A., Shafiq, M. D., & Abdul Hamid, Z. A. (2022). Flame Retardant Coatings: Additives, Binders, and Fillers. Polymers, 14(14), 2911. https://doi.org/10.3390/polym14142911

Mokhtari, M., & Vahid, H. (2016). Salt and its Role in Health and Disease Prevention from the Perspectives of Iranian Medicine and Modern Medicine. Iranian journal of medical sciences, 41(3 Suppl), S58.

Morris, R. (2018, July 9). The Best Poison Ivy Remedies: Soaps, Creams, and More. Healthline. https://www.healthline.com/health/outdoor-health/poison-ivy-remedies

Nall, R. (2013, November 15). Vaginal Pain: Causes, Risk Factors, and Treatment. Healthline. https://www.healthline.com/health/vaginal-pain

Nall, R. (2018, August 24). Natural Wart Removal Tips. Healthline. https://www.healthline.com/health/natural-wart-removal#natural-treatments

Nall, R. (2019, July 17). 26 Uses for Rubbing Alcohol, Plus What You Shouldn't Use It For. Healthline; Healthline Media. https://www.healthline.com/health/rubbing-alcohol-uses

National Center for Complementary and Integrative Health. (2020, October). Peppermint Oil. NCCIH. https://www.nccih.nih.gov/health/peppermint-oil

National Center for Complementary and Integrative Health. (2020, August). Licorice Root. NCCIH. https://www.nccih.nih.gov/health/licorice-root

Nicotine Keeps Leaf-Loving Herbivores at Bay. (2004). PLoS Biology, 2(8), e250. https://doi.org/10.1371/journal.pbio.0020250

# References

Nolden, A. A., Lenart, G., & Hayes, J. E. (2019). Putting out the fire – Efficacy of common beverages in reducing oral burn from capsaicin. Physiology & behavior, 208, 112557. https://doi.org/10.1016/j.physbeh.2019.05.018

Nunez, K. (2021, November 23). How to Make Soap from Scratch. Healthline. https://www.healthline.com/health/how-to-make-soap

Nunez, K. (2022, February 23). 16 Home Remedies for Warts You Can Try Today. Healthline. https://www.healthline.com/health/home-remedies-for-warts

O'Brien, S. (2020, November 11). 7 Science-Based Benefits of MCT Oil. Healthline. https://www.healthline.com/nutrition/mct-oil-benefits

Peedikayil, F. C., Sreenivasan, P., & Narayanan, A. (2015). Effect of coconut oil in plaque related gingivitis – A preliminary report. Nigerian medical journal : journal of the Nigeria Medical Association, 56(2), 143–147. https://doi.org/10.4103/0300-1652.153406

Putra, I. B., Jusuf, N. K., & Dewi, N. K. (2022). Skin Changes and Safety Profile of Topical Products During Pregnancy. The Journal of clinical and aesthetic dermatology, 15(2), 49–57.

Petre, A. (2017, June 29). What Is Activated Charcoal Good For? Benefits and Uses. Healthline; Healthline Media. https://www.healthline.com/nutrition/activated-charcoal

Pointer, K. (2017, March 7). Why Do Mosquito Bites Itch? Plus 10 Tips for Itch Relief. Healthline. https://www.healthline.com/health/why-mosquito-bites-itch

Ramalingam, S., Graham, C., Dove, J., Morrice, L., & Sheikh, A. (2020). Hypertonic saline nasal irrigation and gargling should be considered as a treatment option for COVID-19. Journal of global health, 10(1), 010332. https://doi.org/10.7189/jogh.10.010332

Richmond, S. J., Gunadasa, S., Bland, M., & Macpherson, H. (2013). Copper bracelets and magnetic wrist straps for rheumatoid arthritis--analgesic and anti-inflammatory effects: a randomised double-blind placebo controlled crossover trial. PloS one, 8(9), e71529. https://doi.org/10.1371/journal.pone.0071529

Rodak, K., Kokot, I., & Kratz, E. M. (2021). Caffeine as a Factor Influencing the Functioning of the Human Body-Friend or Foe?. Nutrients, 13(9), 3088. https://doi.org/10.3390/nu13093088

# References


Rohrich, C., Plackett, T. P., Scholz, B. M., & Hetzler, M. R. (2019). Proficiency in Improvised Tourniquets for Extremities: A Review. Journal of special operations medicine : a peer reviewed journal for SOF medical professionals, 19(3), 123-127. https://doi.org/10.55460/5XTW-C355

Samidah, S., Prihantono, Ahmad, M., Jompa, J., Rafiah, S., & Usman, A. N. (2021). The effectiveness of 7% table salt concentration test to increase collagen in the healing process of wound. Gaceta sanitaria, 35 Suppl 2, S199-S201. https://doi.org/10.1016/j.gaceta.2021.07.015

Salyer, J. (2016, March). 9 Healthy Benefits of Drinking Aloe Vera Juice. Healthline; Healthline Media. https://www.healthline.com/health/food-nutrition/aloe-vera-juice-benefits

Sanchez-Ramos J. R. (2020). The rise and fall of tobacco as a botanical medicine. Journal of herbal medicine, 22, 100374. https://doi.org/10.1016/j.hermed.2020.100374

Scapagnini, G., Davinelli, S., Di Renzo, L., De Lorenzo, A., Olarte, H. H., Micali, G., Cicero, A. F., & Gonzalez, S. (2014). Cocoa bioactive compounds: significance and potential for the maintenance of skin health. Nutrients, 6(8), 3202-3213. https://doi.org/10.3390/nu6083202

Seladi-Schulman, J. (2019, April 25). About Peppermint Oil Uses and Benefits. Healthline; Healthline Media. https://www.healthline.com/health/benefits-of-peppermint-oil

Shrimanker I, Bhattarai S. Electrolytes. [Updated 2023 Jul 24]. In: StatPearls [Internet]. Treasure Island (FL): StatPearls Publishing; 2024 Jan-. Available from: https://www.ncbi.nlm.nih.gov/books/NBK541123/

Sidhu, P., Shankargouda, S., Rath, A., Hesarghatta Ramamurthy, P., Fernandes, B., & Kumar Singh, A. (2020). Therapeutic benefits of liquorice in dentistry. Journal of Ayurveda and integrative medicine, 11(1), 82-88. https://doi.org/10.1016/j.jaim.2017.12.004

Silver, N. (2017, June 2). How to Get Rid of Hives: 15 Ways. Healthline. https://www.healthline.com/health/skin-disorders/how-to-get-rid-of-hives

Smith A. P. (2016). Chewing gum and stress reduction. Journal of clinical and translational research, 2(2), 52-54.

Songsantiphap, Chankiat, and Pravit Asawanonda. "Topical 15% Zinc Oxide Ointment Significantly Reduces the Size of Common Warts After Four Weeks: A Randomized, Triple-blinded, Placebo-controlled Trial." The Journal of clinical and aesthetic dermatology vol. 12,9 (2019): 26-31.

# References

Spritzler, F. (2019, November 3). Is Carbonated (Sparkling) Water Good or Bad? Healthline. https://www.healthline.com/nutrition/carbonated-water-good-or-bad

Stanborough, R. J. (2019, November 13). 22 Hydrogen Peroxide Uses You Can Try Today. Healthline. https://www.healthline.com/health/hydrogen-peroxide-uses

Streit, L. (2018, September 27). Micronutrients: Types, Functions, Benefits and More. Healthline. https://www.healthline.com/nutrition/micronutrients

Streit, L. (2022, January 5). Does Chocolate Relieve Period Cramps? Healthline. https://www.healthline.com/nutrition/does-chocolate-help-cramps

Sutton, J. (2019, July 29). Homemade Bug Spray: Natural Recipes for Your Skin, Home, and Plants. Healthline. https://www.healthline.com/health/homemade-bug-spray

The Benefits of Having a Healthy Relationship with Chocolate. (n.d.). Www.hopkinsmedicine.org. https://www.hopkinsmedicine.org/health/wellness-and-prevention/the-benefits-of-having-a-healthy-relationship-with-chocolate#:~:text=Increases%20heart%20health%3A%20The%20antioxidants

The Healthline Editorial Team. (2017). 14 Benefits and Uses for Tea Tree Oil. Healthline. https://www.healthline.com/nutrition/tea-tree-oil

The National Cancer Institute. (2014, April 21). Can Taking Aspirin Help Prevent Cancer? - NCI. Www.cancer.gov. https://www.cancer.gov/about-cancer/causes-prevention/research/aspirin-cancer-risk#:~:text=The%20study%2C%20led%20by%20Dr

Van De Walle, G. (2021, September 30). What Is Citric Acid, and Is It Bad for You? Healthline. https://www.healthline.com/nutrition/citric-acid

Vandergriendt, C. (2020, August 20). Rubbing Alcohol vs. Hydrogen Peroxide for Disinfecting. Healthline. https://www.healthline.com/health/rubbing-alcohol-vs-hydrogen-peroxide

Villalba, H., & Abbas, M. A. (2007). Hemorrhoids: modern remedies for an ancient disease. The Permanente journal, 11(2), 74-76. https://doi.org/10.7812/tpp/06-156

Waqas, M. K., Khan, B. A., Akhtar, N., Chowdhry, F., Khan, H., Bakhsh, S., Khan, S., & Rasul, A. (2017). Fabrication of Tamarindus indica seeds extract loaded-cream for photo-aged skin: Visioscan® studies. Postepy dermatologii i alergologii, 34(4), 339-345. https://doi.org/10.5114/ada.2017.69314

# References

Water Treatment Chemical Supply Chain Profile – Hydrogen Peroxide. (n.d.). In EPA.gov (p. 2). EPA.gov. https://www.epa.gov/system/files/documents/2023-03/Hydrogen%20Peroxide%20Supply%20Chain%20Profile.pdf

Watson, K. (2017, December 6). Is Gargling Hydrogen Peroxide Effective and Safe? Healthline; Healthline Media. https://www.healthline.com/health/gargling-hydrogen-peroxide

Welsh, E. J., Bara, A., Barley, E., & Cates, C. J. (2010). Caffeine for asthma. The Cochrane database of systematic reviews, 2010(1), CD001112. https://doi.org/10.1002/14651858.CD001112.pub2

Whelan, C. (2019, November 19). Vicks for Earache: Does It Work and Should You Use It? Healthline. https://www.healthline.com/health/vicks-for-earache

Whelan, C. (2022, February 23). 7 Causes for a False-Positive Pregnancy Test. Healthline. https://www.healthline.com/health/pregnancy/false-positive-pregnancy-test

White , A. (2017, October 16). Essential Oils for Bug Bites: 7 Oils for Relief. Healthline. https://www.healthline.com/health/essential-oil-for-bug-bites

wikiHow. (2017, September 4). Make Activated Charcoal. WikiHow; wikiHow. https://www.wikihow.com/Make-Activated-Charcoal

wikiHow. How to Melt Plastic. (2024, April 5). WikiHow. https://www.wikihow.com/Melt-Plastic

Yang, R., Yuan, B. C., Ma, Y. S., Zhou, S., & Liu, Y. (2017). The anti-inflammatory activity of licorice, a widely used Chinese herb. Pharmaceutical biology, 55(1), 5-18. https://doi.org/10.1080/13880209.2016.1225775

Zare Javid, A., Bazyar, H., Gholinezhad, H., Rahimlou, M., Rashidi, H., Salehi, P., & Haghighi-Zadeh, M. H. (2019). The effects of ginger supplementation on inflammatory, antioxidant, and periodontal parameters in type 2 diabetes mellitus patients with chronic periodontitis under non-surgical periodontal therapy. A double-blind, placebo-controlled trial. Diabetes, metabolic syndrome and obesity : targets and therapy, 12, 1751-1761. https://doi.org/10.2147/DMSO.S214333

Zore, G., Thakre, A., Abdulghani, M., Bhosle, K., Shelar, A., Patil, R., Kharat, K., & Karuppayil, S. (2022). Menthol Inhibits Candida albicans Growth by Affecting the Membrane Integrity Followed by Apoptosis. Evidence-based complementary and alternative medicine : eCAM, 2022, 1297888. https://doi.org/10.1155/2022/1297888

www.ingramcontent.com/pod-product-compliance
Lightning Source LLC
LaVergne TN
LVHW070422170826
845679LV00035BA/1786

*9798990304208*